Foreign Direct Investment in Large-Scale Agriculture in Africa

T0300088

This book examines environmental sustainability and inclusive economic growth, providing in-depth analysis of foreign direct investment (FDI) in large-scale agriculture in Ethiopia.

In most African states, arable land and other natural resources play a pivotal role in economic growth and development. Ethiopia is one of those countries where agriculture is the backbone of the economy. This sector has also been an attraction for FDI in sub-Saharan Africa since the global food and financial crisis of 2007 and 2008. This book uses six foreign investments in large-scale agriculture as case studies to examine current Ethiopian policies, the patterns of investment they promote, how these impact on land-based resources and communities' well-being. Presenting analyses of the economic, social, environmental and political realities of foreign direct investment in the local context, *Foreign Direct Investment in Large-Scale Agriculture in Africa* discusses how the fundamental principles of pro-poor and environmentally sustainable investments intersect with the government's ambition to advance Ethiopia's development agenda.

This book will be of interest to scholars and students of African economics and sustainable development, African policy makers, intergovernmental organisations as well as multilateral and bilateral development partners

Atkeyelsh G. M. Persson is a programme management officer at the United Nations Economic Commission for Africa, Addis Ababa, Ethiopia.

Routledge Contemporary Africa Series

For more information about this series, please visit: www.routledge.com/Routledge-Contemporary-Africa/book-series/RCAFR

Foreign Direct Investment in Large-Scale Agriculture in Africa

Economic, Social and Environmental Sustainability in Ethiopia

Atkeyelsh G. M. Persson

Routledge
Taylor & Francis Group

LONDON AND NEW YORK

First published 2019 by Routledge

2 Park Square, Milton Park, Abingdon, Oxon, OX14 4RN

605 Third Avenue, New York, NY 10017

Routledge is an imprint of the Taylor & Francis Group, an informa business

First issued in paperback 2020

British Library Cataloguing-in-Publication Data
A catalogue record for this book is available from the British Library

Library of Congress Cataloging-in-Publication Data
Names: Persson, Atkeyelsh G. M., author.
Title: Foreign direct investment in large-scale agriculture in
   Africa : economic, social and environmental sustainability in
   Ethiopia / Atkeyelsh G. M. Persson.
Description: New York : Routledge, 2019. | Series: Routledge
   contemporary Africa series ; 15 | Includes bibliographical references.
Identifiers: LCCN 2019002503 (print) | LCCN 2019015430 (ebook) |
   ISBN 9780429020018 (Ebook) | ISBN 9780429672286 (Adobe
   Reader) | ISBN 9780429670794 (Epub) | ISBN 9780429669309
   (Mobipocket) | ISBN 9780367030360 (hardback)
Subjects: LCSH: Agricultural development projects—Ethiopia. |
   Investments, Foreign—Ethiopia. | Ethiopia—Economic policy.
Classification: LCC HC845.Z9 (ebook) | LCC HC845.Z9 E4468 2019
   (print) | DDC 338.96309051—dc23
LC record available at https://lccn.loc.gov/2019002503

ISBN: 978-0-367-03036-0 (hbk)
ISBN: 978-0-367-78634-2 (pbk)

Typeset in Times New Roman
by Apex CoVantage, LLC

Contents

Figures

Tables

Acronyms and abbreviations

ADLI	Agricultural development–led industrialisation
AfDB	African Development Bank
AU	African Union
AUC	African Union Commission
BBC	British Broadcasting Corporation
BITs	Bilateral investment agreements
CGIAR	Consultative Group on International Agricultural Research
EAILAA	Ethiopian Agricultural Investment Land Administration Agency
EMSAU	Environmental Management and Social Affairs Unit
E&SIA	Environmental and Social Impact Assessment
EGP	Ethiopian Government Portal
EIA	Environmental Impact Assessment
EIC	Ethiopian Investment Commission
EMU	Environmental Management Unit
EPA	Environmental Protection Authority
EPLF	Eritrean People's Liberation Force
EPRDF	Ethiopian People's Revolutionary Democratic Front
EPZs	Export-processing zones
ETIA	Ethiopian Investment Agency
F&G	Framework and guidelines
FAO	Food and Agriculture Organization of the United Nations
FDI	Foreign direct investment
GAO	Government Accountability Office
GDP	Gross domestic product
GTP	Growth and Transformation Plan
GRARDB	Gambella Regional Agricultural and Rural Development Bureau
HIV/AIDS	Human Immunodeficiency Virus Infection and Acquired Immune Deficiency Syndrome
HoA-REC/N	Horn of Africa Regional Environment Centre and Network
IFAD	International Fund for Agricultural Development
IMF	International Monetary Fund
IOM	International Organization for Migration
IWMI	International Water Management Institute

LUP	Land-use planning
MNEs	Multinational enterprises
MoFED	Ministry of Finance and Economic Development
MoI	Ministry of Information
MoLSA	Ministry of Labour and Social Affairs
NPC	National Planning Commission
OLI	Ownership advantage, Locations advantage, Internalize of operations
PAs	Peasant associations
PCs	Producers' cooperatives
PLC	Private limited company
PLUP	Participatory land-use planning
PPESA	Privatisation and Public Enterprises Supervising Agency
SEA	Strategic Environmental Assessment
SIMP	Socio-economic Impact Management Plan
SNNPR	Southern Nations and Nationalities of People
SSA	Sub-Saharan Africa
TPLF	Tigray People Liberation Front
TUAC	Trade Union Advisory Committee
UDHR	Universal Declaration of Human Rights
UN	United Nations
UNCTAD	United Nations Conference on Trade and Development
UNECA	United Nations Economic Commission for Africa
UNEP	United Nations Environment Programme
UNHCR	United Nations High Commissioner for Refugees
US	United States

Acknowledgements

Many people, both in Addis Ababa and in the case study regions, assisted me in collecting data for this research. I am thankful to all of them. In particular, I would like to express my sincere thanks to key informants for their time and for sharing with me their invaluable and candid views, without which this would not have been achieved. Reading materials that served as inputs for this work were accessed from different organisations and individuals. I remain grateful to them for that.

1 Introduction

1.1 Background

1.1.1 The 'Africa-rising' narrative

Since 2000, Africa-rising narrative has been the centre of global discussion in various communication platforms such as big international conferences, media (*The Economist*, *Financial Times*, British Broadcasting Corporation [BBC]), economic research institutions, and intergovernmental organisations such as the United Nations (UN), the World Bank and the International Monetary Fund (IMF). This phenomenon of good economic performance has been the argument for many African countries governments, including Ethiopia, to get praised by the international community. This economic performance is based on gross domestic product (GDP) growth; rising per capita income; rising government investment in infrastructure; rising investment in other sectors of the economy, especially agriculture and minerals and trade; the rising number of billionaires in Africa; and the rapid growth of rural–urban migration and urbanisation in cities like Addis Ababa and Nairobi.

However, there are a number of queries with regard to the Africa-rising narrative: What empirical evidence supports this Africa-rising narrative? What are the intellectual arguments pro and against this narrative? How can it be teased from the "good economic" assessment model? Are the good economic performance indicators alone able to measure Africa's sustainable development without having the social and environmental components? Can the Africa-rising narrative be accurate while there are huge inequalities among the citizenry? How long would this narrative continue knowing that the economies of many African countries are dependent on agricultural commodity and minerals export, whose global price fluctuate tremendously?

Hence, this book is an attempt to respond to the questions by looking at the agricultural sector which is the backbone of many African countries economy. This sector has also been an attraction for foreign direct investment (FDI) in sub-Saharan Africa (SSA) since the global food and financial crisis of 2007 and 2008. In order to demonstrate the Africa-rising narrative and show empirical evidence, Ethiopia's case is examined. The government of Ethiopia, like many other African countries' governments, strongly advocates for FDI in large-scale agriculture so as to advance agricultural transformation including ensuring food security to its people. Evidence shows that Ethiopia has kept a two-digit growth of GDP since 2000 which is due mainly to the agricultural sector (World Bank, 2016). This GDP growth for 10 consecutive years made "Ethiopia Rising" story which has been shared widely.

Critics, however, say that the "Africa/Ethiopia rising" narrative is one-dimensional and focusing on economic growth while it ignores the two fundamental elements for sustainable development (i.e. social development and environmental sustainability). It also stresses that the current high-growth rate in Africa neither is sustainable as it is heavily dependent on the export of primary commodities (i.e. agricultural and extractive industry) nor has generated sufficient productive employment, improved living conditions or a decline in poverty and inequality. The lack of economic diversification, which contributed to the rapid urbanisation, and increased population growth while resources are shrinking, compounded with the threat of climate change, undermine the Africa-rising narrative. This economic growth benefits only small segments of the population such as political elites and foreign investors. This could trigger more competition over resources and conflict. There is, therefore, a need to diversify African economies to absorb the massive youth population entering the job market each year and to make growth inclusive and sustainable, as well as to make the Africa-rising narrative complete.

1.1.2 The importance of FDI in agricultural land in Africa

In most, if not all, African states' land occupies the centre of social, political and economic life. It also has important historical, cultural and spiritual meanings. Land and natural resources play a pivotal role in economic growth and development in African countries as many of them rely heavily on agriculture and natural resources for their GDP, employment, national food needs and export revenue (UNECA, 2006). About 60% of the African population relies on farming and livestock production for their livelihood and income. In developing nations, such as those in Africa, millions of women are engaged in farm work and contribute to family food security and nutrition, supplementary incomes, national agricultural output and the natural environment (Hanstad et al., 2004; Gazdar and Quan, 2004; Quisumbing, 1994; AUC-AfDB-UNECA, 2010). In countries such as Ethiopia, the agricultural sector contributes about 45% of the GDP, 86% of foreign currency earnings, 85% of employment and 70% of raw materials for local industries (ETIA, 2013; EGP, 2016). In Africa, although there are plenty of fertile and high-value lands, population growth and the development of the land market are creating pressure and competition on those lands (AUC-AfDB-UNECA, 2007). As evidenced in many African states, land rights allocated to and exercised by the state often clash with land-tenure practices of citizens. As such, land tenure is insecure for many people in Africa. It is, in turn, a major problem in the development of large- and small-scale land-based investments (AUC-AfDB-UNECA, 2007).

1.1.3 Views on FDI in large-scale agriculture in Africa

There are divergent views regarding FDI in large-scale agriculture; some are for and others are against promoting the investment. The debates on the issue grow stronger as both the demand and supply sides of FDI in large-scale agriculture continued to grow. The following subsections highlight the different views on FDI in large-scale agriculture.

1.1.3.1 Arguments for FDI in large-scale agriculture

Scholars who argue for FDI state that it plays an important role in fostering economic growth, transferring technology, creating employment, supplementing domestic investment, increasing domestic competition, increasing wages, enhancing the capacity of people in developing countries and bringing other positive externalities (TeVelde, 2001; Kim, 2003, 2011).The Food and Agriculture Organisation (FAO, 2001), Amani et al. (2003) and Elibariki (2007) further substantiate FDI's important role in increasing productivity and agricultural growth, which are directly linked to improving the living conditions of the poor by bridging the investment and technological gap faced by the poor. These scholars stress that in low-income countries, the per capita decline of arable land, high production costs and rapid population growth threaten the attainment of agricultural sector development. Hence, the FDI flow in the agricultural sector of these countries, especially those dependent on agriculture such as Ethiopia, is necessary to acquire the required agricultural inputs in order to increase productivity and achieve sustainable growth and poverty reduction.

1.1.3.2 Arguments against FDI in large-scale agriculture

Scholars who argue against FDI claim that FDI in large-scale agriculture spells disaster for rural people and for the health of river systems (Oakland Institute, 2011). In Africa, about 70% of arable land has recently been taken over by foreign investors for agricultural production (World Bank, 2010). These investments have been taking place under the pretext of modernising agriculture and expanding African economies (Steve, 2011). This has huge implications for other scarce land-based resources such as water. It removes the control and use of core natural resources from the local African people, whose livelihoods were formerly dependent on these resources. This phenomenon is threatening the food security, water security, income and cultural integrity of local people (Steve, 2011). Large-scale land acquisition can also pose environmental risks, such as biodiversity loss (AUC-AfDB-UNECA, 2011) and increased reliance on aid (Oakland Institute, 2011).

1.2 Why this book and what it is about

By the same token with the 'Africa-rising' hype, the 'Ethiopia-rising' narrative, which has been the discourse in the national, regional and international development debates, is based only on the two-digit economic growth that made Ethiopia one of the fastest-growing economies. Furthermore, the government of Ethiopia strongly advocates for FDI in large-scale agriculture so as to advance rural & agricultural transformation, which is the ultimate goal of the government, as well as to make Ethiopia a middle-income economy by 2025. This is demonstrated in its investment policies and strategies, as well as institutions, established to promote FDI in large-scale agriculture. These include the development of infrastructure, the provision of health services (especially the control of malaria in lowland areas where there is abundant land) and the upgrading of the skills of agricultural labour. Sections 5.4, 6.2 and 6.3 discuss in detail the reasons why the government of Ethiopia supports FDI, especially in large-scale agriculture, as well as the mechanism put into place to facilitate FDI.

At the same time, critics say that these investments are not pro-poor or environmentally sustainable. The existing studies on this issue do not provide detailed data on the extent, nature and impacts of these investments in Ethiopia. The available data lack sufficient detail to determine whether these investments are environmentally, socially and economically viable or not. This could be due to the fact that the investments are occurring at a fast pace, especially after the 2007 global food crisis which was followed by a financial crisis. It could also be that the issue is politically sensitive and confidentiality issues hinder access to data. This information gap on the FDI in large-scale agriculture in Ethiopia demands an in-depth study on the extent and impact of these investments in Ethiopia.

Although this book admits the dilemma of the Ethiopian government to achieve economic growth while protecting the environment, it argues that the 'Ethiopia-rising' narrative is incomplete as it based only on GDP growth and disregards the two fundamental pillars of sustainable development (i.e. social and environment). The book substantiates its argument by presenting the results of in-depth case studies of FDI in large-scale agriculture in Ethiopia and the discussion and implications of the results with reference to the features and fundamental principles of pro-poor and environmentally sustainable investments, on one hand, and the government's ambition to advance Ethiopia's development agenda, on the other. It is also with the view to inform those interested in improving FDI in large-scale agriculture in Africa while contributing to the body of knowledge in this area.

The book is cognisant of the two case study regions, namely Gambella and Beneshangul-Gumuz, are not representatives of Ethiopia in terms of the overall FDI flow in other sectors and the contributions to the overall GDP of the country. However, they have the largest share of FDI in large-scale agriculture in Ethiopia (see Chapter 7 for a detailed discussion). Furthermore, agriculture is the backbone of the Ethiopian economy which contributes to about 45% of the GDP. The argument on Ethiopia-rising narrative to be based only GDP growth is still valid.

1.3 Theoretical and methodological highlights

1.3.1 Theoretical framework

The famous "Dunning's eclectic paradigm", which is a holistic model applied to assess a company's strategy to expand its operations through FDI, is not suitable for this book on its own as this book is about FDI in large-scale agriculture and it covers not only FDI economics but also social, environmental and political aspects. Hence, the theoretical framework of this book is critical realism, which allows the use of other paradigms, such as positivism, critical theory and social constructivism, which are necessary for research in FDI, agriculture and land tenure.

Critical realism paradigm enables showing the real event (i.e. FDI in large-scale agriculture in Ethiopia) and revealing the hidden economic, social and political reality, as well as the investment to be understood in the local context.

Furthermore, FDI in large-scale agriculture differs from FDI in the manufacturing or service sectors. As such, the main driving force for this investment is food security, among other things. This underpinning issue of food security for both home and host countries that is encompassed in these investments is discussed in detail in Sections 3.4 and 5.2.1. In addition, Sections 1.1.2, 1.1.3.2, 2.3, 5.2.8, 6.3.2, 7.2, 7.3.2, 7.4 and 8.1 discuss the issue of food security related to FDI in large-scale agriculture.

1.3.2 Research methodology

This book analyzes previous studies on FDI, agriculture and land tenure and identifies the relevance of case study research methodology to this book. The case study method is suitable for in-depth investigations (Yin, 2003), which is required to bridge the identified information gap on FDI in large-scale agriculture in Ethiopia. In addition, FDI in large-scale agriculture is a complex issue that involves economic, social, political, environmental and cultural aspects and requires a multifaceted methodology rich in contextual analysis. It needs to be examined and analyzed in its specific environment of occurrence. Case study methodology, therefore, enables this book to conduct an in-depth empirical investigation of the FDI in large-scale agriculture in Ethiopia being pro-poor and environmentally sustainable within its real-life context using multiple sources of evidence such as interviews including focus group discussion (see Appendix 1 for the coded list of interviewees), review of documents (see Appendix 2 for the list of official documents used) and direct observation (see Appendix 3 for the observation checklist). The chosen methodology is compatible with the critical realism paradigm, which is the theoretical ground of this book.

For this book, multiple case studies were conducted in order to make the collection, construction and analysis of the empirical data rigorous and increase the robustness of the study. This book admits the difficulties of reporting from an objective standpoint; therefore, it applies critical thinking skills, and each case is evaluated methodically to enable the author to remove the impact of any personal bias. The primary target audience of this book's findings include African, especially Ethiopian, policy makers and policy implementers at all levels of government, followed by foreign investors, local communities, research institutions and development partners such as UN entities, bilateral and multilateral donors, as well as the public who are interested in this matter. The author is aware of these diverse audiences, and so the analysis for this book is prepared to cater to a variety of readers. Chapter 4 provides detail on the research methodology.

1.4 Organisation of the book

This book is organised under nine chapters, including the Introduction, which constitutes this first chapter. To give some background issues, the chapter starts by situating the performance of the agricultural sector, which is the backbone of the economies of many African countries, in the 'Africa-rising' narrative of the present decade. It also traverses the importance of, and views on, FDI in agriculture; the purposes of the book; and theoretical and methodological highlights about FDI in large-scale agriculture. Issues about and the knowledge base of FDI are presented in Chapter 2, which focuses on theoretical bases, research on and determinants of inward FDI.

Chapter 3 dwells on FDI and agriculture, with a focus on agricultural transformation strategies, investors in, and drivers and impacts of, FDI in large-scale agriculture. The chapter further discusses the features and fundamental principles of pro-poor and environmentally sustainable investment in large-scale agriculture, as well as frameworks and guidelines to assess investment policies. The research methodology is discussed in the fourth chapter. The history and nature of FDI in Ethiopian agriculture are presented in the fifth chapter, which takes us through the issue during the imperial, the Dergue (the military) and Ethiopian People's Revolutionary Democratic Front (EPRDF) regimes and then draws similarities, differences and implications of the agricultural investment policies of the three regimes. Chapter 6 threads through policies, strategies and institutions that promote FDI in large-scale agriculture in Ethiopia; the terms, conditions, content and intent of agricultural land-lease agreements; and practical challenges in implementing the policies that promote FDI in large-scale agriculture in Ethiopia.

Chapter 7 describes six case study projects and characterises the communities surrounding those projects in Gambella and Beneshangul-Gumuz national regional states of Ethiopia, while Chapter 8 presents an analysis of the case studies and their results and discussion and implications of the findings. The book ends with conclusions and recommendations that are captured in Chapter 9.

2 The knowledge base of FDI

2.1 Introduction

Chapter 1 presented the introduction to the study, which runs through the background, the purposes/rationales that necessitated this book, the methodological highlights and information on the organisation of the book. This second chapter presents issues and the knowledge base about FDI in general through a reflective synthesis of the pertinent conceptual and empirical literature.

2.2 Theoretical bases of FDI research

FDI theory is based on several integrative theories such as international capital market theory, firm theory and the theory of international trade (Popovici and Călin, 2014; Nayak and Choudhury, 2014). Nayak and Choudhury (2014) further elaborate the theories of FDI based on perfect competition, imperfect markets and strength of investor's country currency. These theories are grounded by the FDI variables, namely ownership advantage, location advantage and internalise of operations (Dunning, 2000; Popovici and Călin, 2014; Nayak and Choudhury, 2014). This triumvirate, O-L-I-, is called the eclectic paradigm (see Section 1.3). Some scholars argue that the location theories, especially institutional variables, are the core of the investment decision-making process for inward FDI (Boman and Hellqvist, 2012; Popovici and Călin, 2014).

From the host country's stance, FDI is presumed to free up financial, goods and factor markets (Te Velde, 2001; Moosa, 2002); also, it is the least volatile source of international investment for host countries (Lipsey, 1999). In addition, FDI is perceived as a means for channelling resources to developing countries, as well as for playing an important role in the economic transformation of these countries through its complements to domestic saving, increasing foreign earnings and increasing total investment in the host economy (Moosa, 2002). Nayak and Choudhury (2014) acknowledge that the theories of FDI have mainly focused on the movements of investment from developed countries to other countries, and it fails to capture the recent trend of investment from developing nations, such as India, to others.

FDI is assumed to transfer technology and know-how, as well as facilitate access to export markets (Kim, 2003, 2011). These economic effects of FDI are widely recognised. Nowadays, the political, social and cultural effects of FDI are being noticed, especially by citizens of the host country (Moose, 2002). These effects include a loss of national sovereignty due to its inherent influencing power and the creation of the foreign investors' own territories in the host country (i.e. symbolises new colonialism and expansion of foreign elites in the host country), as well as an insensitive attitude to the customs of the host country's local population (Moose, 2002). Nayak and Choudhury (2014) stress that the theories of FDI have different approaches, but all of them have a common view that an investor moves abroad to reap the benefits of the advantages described by the Dunning's eclectic paradigm.

2.3 Research on FDI in large-scale agriculture

Hallam (2009) argues that FDI in agriculture in developing countries is not a new occurrence. This is confirmed by Brown (2013) who states that large-scale agricultural investments with the foreign investors being industrial countries to produce tropical products (such as sugarcane, tea and bananas) have been practised the past 150 years. However, the new trend of FDI in large-scale agriculture is to produce basic food (such as wheat, rice, corn and soybeans) and biofuels to be exported to the investing country. In addition, this new type of foreign investment focuses on the acquisition of agricultural land rather than creating joint ventures with local investors (Brown, 2013; Hallam, 2009). This argument is supported in the studies of Schüpbach (2014) and Consultative Group on International Agricultural Research (CGIAR; 2014). Cotula and Vermeulen (2009) further elaborate on the recent increase of FDI in large-scale agriculture in Africa. They reveal that since the mid-2000s, large tracts of land have been allocated for foreign investors in Ethiopia, Ghana, Madagascar and Mali. They further reveal that 1.6 million hectares of land, extendable to 2.7 million hectares, has been earmarked by the government of Ethiopia for commercial farm investors (Cotula and Vermeulen, 2009).

Metcalfe and Kepe (2008) argue that the recent increase of FDI in large-scale agriculture has the potential to contribute effectively to local livelihoods and may help to address the urgent need for food security in Africa. In addition, FDI in the agricultural sector could stimulate development and reduction of hunger. This argument is reinforced by Chari (2004), who highlights the benefits of FDI in agriculture. Chari (2004) stresses the importance of having an efficient and effective agricultural FDI policy in place. This could unleash latent potential, strengthen the host country's food security and improve livelihoods of the local community and safeguard the environment. Adequate institutions should be established to promote property rights and facilitate local community engagement when considering deals with investors in order to promote transparency and protect the environment (Chari, 2004).

There are, however, questions about these huge agricultural land deals, especially regarding transparency and checks and balances, especially for state-owned land. These are important as the community's land-use right is already insecure due to inaccessible registration procedures and legislative gaps (Cotula and Vermeulen, 2009; Metcalfe and Kepe, 2008). Gerlach and Liu (2010) conducted case studies in Uganda, Mali, Madagascar, Sudan, Morocco, Ghana, Senegal and Egypt. These reveal that the legal framework and procedures governing land acquisition, land registration, land use and the rights of smallholder farmers are generally unclear and lacking in transparency. Karlsson (2012) confirms the preceding claims and reveals that expropriation laws are generally ambiguous, allowing governments to misuse them to seize land and related properties for private investment purposes.

Cotula and Vermeulen (2009), as well as Metcalfe and Kepe (2008), argue that local community participation in the negotiations of these investments is absent and their interests in land, water and other resources are not considered when agricultural lands are allocated for investors. They conclude that land has been leased to foreign investors without consulting with the local community. This conclusion is supported in a study by the Global Policy Forum (2012) that states that FDI in land may possibly be negotiated at the highest political level between the governments of investor and host countries. Djire et al. (2012) confirm this in the case of the Malibya agriculture investment. The Libyan and the Malian governments agreed on Libyan investment in the Malian Niger Office Area to produce food for the Libyan population (Djire et al., 2012). FDI of the South Korean company Daewoo Logistics in Madagascar is an example of a private company involved in an agreement with the government of Madagascar (*Financial Times*, 2008). The Saudi Arabian company Saudi Star, operating as a private investor in Ethiopia, is another example (Saudi Star's Land Rent Contractual Agreement, 2010).

Cotula and Vermeulen (2009) state that the approved and documented agricultural land deals in Ethiopia are leased and the duration ranges from short term to 99 years. The leased lands, recorded at the national investment promotion agency, are classified as "wastelands" with no prior users despite these lands have been used for seasonal cultivation and grazing. Cotula and Vermeulen (2009) reckon that the lands leased to investors are high-value lands with good rainfall or irrigation potential and high-quality soils.

According to Gerlach and Liu (2010), the impact of FDI on host countries varies from country to country, as well as across locations within a country. The same source also shows that FDI has not generated the expected economic benefits, such as employment creation, higher productivity, technology transfer and enforcement of production standards. The primary purpose of investors' venture into FDI in large-scale agriculture is to respond to food security in the investors' home country and to secure food supply in case food prices rise in the future, as they did in 2007 and 2008. Thus, while investors' pursue their motives, the findings revealed that some of the investment projects displaced local farmers who, along with the land, lost traditional income-generating activities. Considering such revelations, Gerlach and Liu (2010) conclude that the granting of land without undertaking the relevant studies and public consultations to ensure the social, environmental and economic feasibility of an investment project is a critical problem that is likely to have adverse effects on local communities.

Hallam (2009) states that foreign investment in agriculture in Africa, especially in SSA, involves complex and controversial economic, political, institutional, legal and ethical issues in relation to food security, poverty reduction, rural development, technology transfer and access to land and water. The rapid increase of interest in foreign investment in agricultural land in developing countries is of great concern to the international community, and they have called for "responsible investment" and proposed international cooperation to secure it. Tran-Nguyen (2010) confirms the claim and argues that the agricultural products from FDI are not sold or valued by the global markets since they go directly to the investing countries. Hallam (2009) stresses that this arrangement raises several questions with regard to the investment benefits to the host country since the agricultural products are not valued at international prices. The study concludes that, with this arrangement, the benefit to the host country is little or non-existent since it is not sufficient to fully compensate for the loss of food production for domestic consumption, especially in many SSA countries where there are chronic food shortages and where FDI is targeted.

Jimenez (2011) and Lv et al. (2010) state that studies on the current trends of FDI in agricultural land in Africa are limited in number as this could be a new trend occurring at a fast pace. The review of the literature as part of this study also confirms this conclusion, specifically for Ethiopia. Hallam (2009) demonstrates the lack of detailed data on the extent, nature and impacts of foreign investments in agriculture in developing countries. This is due to the sensitivity of the issues surrounding these investments and the need for confidentiality. Country case studies are proposed to investigate the extent and impact of inward investments in order to fully comprehend the issues (Hallam, 2009). One of the objectives of this research is to critically examine the nature, history and impacts of FDI in large-scale agriculture in Ethiopia with the view to bridge the information gap on this issue.

The findings of previous research on similar research questions to this study are presented in the following sections. However, none of these studies have looked at the role of policy in shaping FDI in large-scale agriculture in Ethiopia and the policy implications for the poor and for environmental sustainability. This highlights a gap in knowledge and informs the objective of this study.

2.4 Determinants of inward FDI

Dunning's OLI paradigm is widely accepted and enables foreign investors to decide where to invest (Dunning, 2000). Boman and Hellqvist (2012) emphasise further the location (L) dimension to be the most critical factor to determine where to invest while the ownership (O) and internalise of operations (I) dimensions are firm-specific factors. TeVelde (2001) concludes that a location advantage is not only related to access to natural resources but also the availability of a skilled workforce, infrastructure and local supply services.

Boman and Hellqvist (2012), and TeVelde (2001) distinguish inward FDI as seeking access to a natural resource, market, labour market efficiency and innovation capacity. Each of them has distinct criteria. Boman and Hellqvist (2012) highlight that innovation capacity seeking FDI focuses mainly in developed countries. This claim is supported by Ireland's policy statement on FDI, which states that Ireland is one of the most enterprise-aligned science, technology and innovation systems in the world (Ireland's Department of Jobs, Enterprise and Innovation, July 2014).

2.4.1 Host country policies, regulatory and institutional frameworks

There is a general basic assumption that the positive effects of FDI (i.e. economic growth, skill upgrading and capital) outweigh its negative effects (income inequality, environmental degradation and profit repatriation). This is, however, shown to be true only if appropriate inward FDI policies and regulatory and institutional frameworks are in place and executed consistently and effectively; this requires strong local institutions (TeVelde, 2001). The African Union Commission (AUC)–African Development Bank (AfDB)–UN Economic Commission for Africa (UNECA; 2007) confirmed that the inconsistency of policy, especially pertaining to land tenure, is reflected in many African states' policies resulting in conflict and an additional obstacle to agricultural investment. A study in seven African countries, conducted by Basu and Srinivasan (2002), concludes that a well-designed policy framework should be successful in attracting FDI into Africa and enabling host countries to reap the desired benefits. Sass (2003) reveals that Hungary's FDI policy to quickly build up the local institutions is one of the success factors for the country's inward FDI.

A host country's FDI policy should aim to improve the capacity of employees within institutions promoting FDI in order to serve FDI activities better. This could be in the form of contributing to formal and/or informal education and on-the-job training or employing a relatively more skilled and educated workforce. Hence, the policy needs to identify the skill requirements of FDI at different stages of their operations and to facilitate the required skills accordingly (TeVelde, 2001). The author stresses that host country policies, regulations and institutions should create location advantages, such as skilled workforce, infrastructure and local supply services, in order to attract and make FDI productive and work for the development of a host country (see Sections 2.4.3. and 2.4.4). This argument is confirmed by Sass (2003) in a study of Hungary's FDI policies that have been amended since the 1990s in order to match FDI activities with the country's available skills.

Fan (2002), Kim (2003), Kokko (2003), TeVelde (2001) and Globerman and Chen (2010) underscore the importance of public policy, including government spending in infrastructure, education, training and research and development. This plays a pivotal role in ensuring greatest productivity spillovers and in influencing a favourable inward FDI environment.

Blyde et al. (2004) and Sass (2003) further articulate that export-oriented FDI policy has a significant spillover effect for domestic firms. However, Cheung and Lin (2004) are of the view that there is no significant relationship between the export-orientation and spillover effects of FDI. Globerman and Chen (2010) suggest that geographical concentration matters for the quality of FDI as it encourages technology transfer and knowledge sharing between firms and increases the FDI spillover effect. TeVelde (2001) concludes that host-country FDI policies need to ensure the long-lasting benefits of FDI to the host country through the creation of direct and indirect linkages between FDI and domestic firms.

2.4.2 Political, social and economic stability

Bartels et al. (2008) highlight that inward FDI is attracted by location-related factors such as political and economic stability, a strong regulatory framework and government institutional capacity. A significant number of empirical studies confirm a positive relation among inward FDI, social stability and improved security (Bandelj, 2001; Baniak et al., 2002; Basu and Srinivasan, 2002; Kokko, 2003; Devereux and Sabates-Wheeler, 2004; Bartels et al., 2008; AU, 2008; Adato and Hoddinott, 2008; Mutangadura, 2009; Groh and Wich, 2009; Globerman and Chen, 2010; UN, 2014).

Strengthening of government institutional capacity and delineating their responsibilities is important. This can enhance the sustainability, effectiveness and efficiency of services, thus facilitating the adequate operation of FDI (Williamson, 1979; Killing, 1983; Atkinson and Coleman, 1989; Fiszbein, 1997; Gow et al., 2000; Emery et al., 2000; Loewendahl, 2001; Luo, 2002; Trink, 2007; Masaba et al., 2013; Seyoum, 2009; Bissoon, 2011). North (1990) stresses the significance of quality institutions and highlights the role of services, such as formulating and enforcing contracts. This can positively impact economic activities through the low transaction and production costs. Globerman and Chen (2010) identify that it is very important for local institutions that promote FDI policies to educate foreign investors regarding FDI potential locations and specific economic advantages. They should also foresee potential bottlenecks in administrative procedures and addressing these proactively. Delays that may cause costs and risks for foreign investment could be thus minimised or avoided.

Groh and Wich (2009) conclude that economic activity, the legal and political environment and the business environment are the key factors that determine inward FDI. This conclusion is further strengthened by findings of Basu and Srinivasan (2002) in FDI in Botswana, Namibia, Mauritius, Lesotho, Swaziland, Mozambique and Uganda. They claim that the success of these countries in attracting FDI is partly attributed to political, social and macroeconomic stability. The authors affirm the importance of these factors in attracting inward FDI rather than giving tax incentives, which play an insignificant role in the FDI investment decisions. This view is backed up by Abeasi (2003), who concludes that, in Ghana, incentives to attract FDI are not sufficient and they are only the "icing on the cake". Abeasi (2003) argues that host country governments need to focus on macro indicators such as sound macroeconomic performance and strong institutions.

Globerman and Chen (2010) state that subsidies and tax breaks do not promote FDI in the longer run; it could negatively affect any spillover productivity effects from the investment. They also conclude that lower taxes mean a reduction in the quality and quantity of public services and amenities since these services are paid from taxes. This, in turn, negatively affects FDI's productivity once it is operational in the country. This claim is challenged by Demirhan and Masca (2008), who conclude that low tax rates are one of the important elements for attracting inward FDI to developing countries.

2.4.3 Labour availability and labour market contexts

Banga (2003) reveals that investors from developed and developing countries look for different locational advantages. The determinants for attracting inward FDI from developed countries are large market size, availability of infrastructure and skilled labour while developing countries are attracted by the availability of lower cost of labour rather than skilled labour. The latter claim is refuted by Barrell and Pain (1996), Rodriguez and Pallas (2008) and Demirhan and Masca (2008), who emphasis the importance of a host country's labour productivity for FDI decision-making regardless of the FDI source country. Bartels et al. (2008) are of the view that FDI is attracted by the availability of skilled labour rather than non-productive low labour cost. The authors reveal that unproductivity of labour is one of the reasons for the decrease in FDI inflows in SSA compared to other continents (from 9.55% in 1970 to 2.7% in 2006). However, Janicki and Wunnava (2004) argue that labour costs are the key determinant for inward FDI. Basu and Srinivasan (2002) reveal that a bilingual language environment and skilled and cheap labour force are two factors for the success of Mauritius in attracting FDI.

There are two streams of literature on the relationship between labour standards and FDI. One stream argues that FDI is attracted to where there are low standards of labour and environment, "[r]acing to the bottom" (TUAC, 1995; Sarna, 2005; Javorcik and Spatareanu, 2005; Zampini, 2008; Davies and Vadlamannati, 2011; Olney, 2013; *The Economist*, 2013). This argument is further elaborated by Olney (2013), who analyzes the various types of FDI and concludes that labour-intensive FDI is negatively and significantly affected by stricter labour standards compared to capital-intensive FDI. This finding is further confirmed by Javorcik and Spatareanu (2005), who conclude that labour market flexibility matters more for FDI in labour-intensive sectors than for those in capital-intensive sectors.

The other stream argues that the bulk of the global FDI flows have been to countries with strong employment rights and strict labour market regulations as these are perceived to increase the labour market efficiency and improve the productivity of workers (Kucera, 2001; OECD, 2002a; Daude et al., 2003; Allard and Garot, 2010). The Organisation for Economic Co-operation and Development (OECD; 2002b) study substantiates further the arguments on the positive relation between stricter labour standards and FDI. The study recognises the existence of low labour standards and FDI in many developing countries, especially in the export-processing zones (EPZs). This argument is supported by Zampini (2008), who, in the mid-1990s, identified that the governments of Namibia and Zimbabwe lowered the core labour standards in the EPZ sector to attract FDI.

2.4.4 Infrastructure

The development of infrastructure, such as transportation, communication and electric power, is key to the development of various sectors to advance the social and economic development of a country. Cognisant of this, the Ethiopian Macroeconomic Policy Framework, for instance, stresses the infrastructure sector's important role in contributing to the development of the agricultural and industrial sectors. In addition, the Ethiopian Investment Policy spells out the needed infrastructure for lowland areas, such as Gambella and Beneshangul-Gumuz regional states, where large-scale agricultural investments are encouraged (see Section 6.2.6).

Many scholars, such as Dupasquier and Osakwe (2006), Mengistu and Adams (2007), Demirhan and Masca (2008), Globerman and Chen (2010) and Hailu (2010), argue that the availability of infrastructure, as well as developing countries' governments' engaging directly in infrastructure programmes, plays an important role in attracting inward FDI flows and facilitate its operation.

2.4.5 Environmental standards

There are conflicting views on the relationship between FDI and environmental standards. One view argues that environmental standards encourage inward FDI as they boost investors' confidence, increase their engagement and enhance their reputation and that their products are more easily accepted (UNCTAD, 1993; Esty and Gentry, 1997; Nordström and Vaughan, 1999; Revesz, 1994; Lall, 2000).

The other view argues that FDI is attracted to low environmental standards and lax environmental regulations "the pollution haven or race to the bottom effect", where FDI is increasing in countries that have low environmental regulation compared to home country regulations (GAO, 1990; Moline, 1993; Jha et al., 1999; Mabey and McNally, 1999; Van Beers et al., 1997; Lu and Huang, 2008).

The third view defuses both arguments. It claims that the rigidity or flexibility of environmental regulations in the host country is not a decisive factor for FDI decision-making (Gentry, 1999; Zarsky, 1999). This claim is refuted by Klavens and Zamparutti (1995) and Picciotto (1999), who suggest that many firms consider environmental regulatory frameworks when deciding on the investment location.

2.4.6 Population health

Alsan et al. (2004) report empirical evidence from 74 countries. This confirms that the health of the host country's population significantly affects FDI inflows, especially for low- and middle-income countries. This finding further confirms the notion that health is an integral component of human capital in developing countries. The research of Bloom and Canning (2000) on the direct and indirect impact of health on economic performance highlights the direct effect of health on workers' productivity as healthy workers are less likely to be absent from work because of illness compared to those affected by a disease. The argument for the indirect effect of health on economic performance is further described by Bhargava (2001), who finds this through its contribution to human capital such as education and work experience. Bhargava (2001) underscores that improved health is able to enhance student learning capacity, and healthy workers have lower rates of absenteeism and longer life expectancies that then enable them to acquire more job experience. This is confirmed by Bloom et al. (2004) in East Asian countries. Their high rates of economic growth in the 1970s are mainly due to improved health that contributes to the rapid increase in labour supply and productivity. The significant relationship between a healthy and productive workforce and FDI inflows in developing countries is confirmed by Noorbakhsh et al. (2001), Majeed and Ahmad (2008) and Tandon (2005).

A World Health Organization (WHO) study on macroeconomic and health argues that a healthy labour force and access to health care are dominant factors for attracting inward FDI due to the effect of health on labour productivity, the investor's own health and that of its expatriate employees (WHO, 2001). The interrelationship among health, health care systems and the economy is further substantiated by Ruger et al. (2011). This is also noted by Bloom and Canning (2008), whose large amount of evidence emphasises the effects of malaria on adults and the loss of working days that affects productivity.

Alsan et al. (2004) show that the recent outbreak of Severe Acute Respiratory Syndrome negatively affected China's FDI inflow but reversed once the outbreak was controlled. This is substantiated by the study of Anyanwu and Yameogo (2015) that reveals the decline of FDI inflow to West Africa due to the deadly Ebola outbreak. The authors further distinguish between an outbreak of diseases and lengthier epidemics such as Human Immunodeficiency Virus and Acquired Immune Deficiency Syndrome (HIV/AIDS) and malaria. They stress that the effect of outbreak disease on the FDI inflow is shorter but that epidemics such as HIV/AIDS and malaria have a long-term effect on FDI inflow.

2.4.7 Investment incentives and their application

Clark (2000), Taylor (2000) and Kokko (2003) stress the importance of investment incentives to attract inward FDI. Kokko (2003) argues that incentives have become vital due to globalisation and are effective in attracting FDI inflows, but their efficiency in bringing benefits to a host country, compared to the costs of providing incentives, are not yet clearly established as there are mixed empirical findings of the spillover benefits from FDI. Kokko (2003) also reveals that some host country governments give generous incentives to attract FDI for political motives rather than to promote real local development.

Haaland and Wooton (1999) emphasise that potential host countries compete with each other to attract FDI. This may raise the level of incentives and benefits to foreign investors rather than to the host country. This claim is substantiated by Graymore (2003) who argues that the key causes for FDI's poor performance in the environmental and social domains are the competition between countries to attract FDI. The pressure to offer a favourable investor environment results in the lowering of social and environmental standards and weak enforcement, especially where investors seek cheap labour costs and natural resources. This view is shared by Zarsky (1999), who states that host countries undermine their local/national environmental standards and their enforcement in order to compete globally to attract FDI.

TeVelde (2001), Kokko (2003) and Kim (2003) suggest the effective application of incentives to enable host countries to benefit from FDI. Incentives should be designed to promote activities related to human resources development, research facilitation and the creation of linkages between foreign and domestic firms. Kokko (2003) stresses that incentives should be performance-based and should not be granted prior to investment.

2.4.8 Conditions set by host country: local content requirement

Kumar (2003) highlights the number of theoretical and empirical studies that show that the requirement for local content is one of the most common performance requirements imposed by host countries. This promotes the contribution of FDI to local income and employment generation by FDI as well as the transfer of technology and other spillover effects. For example, Brazil, Mexico and Thailand built highly competitive automobile industries by enforcing and monitoring their local content requirements and export performance requirements for foreign automobile investors.

Kumar (2003) stresses that local content requirements are context-specific. Success depends on various factors such as clarity of policy objectives, the capability of the host government to enforce and monitor policy compliance, the absorptive capacity in terms of local workforce skills and the strength of domestic firms, and other locational advantages (Kumar, 2003). This claim is supported by Balasubramanyam (2003). Picciotto (2003) highlights the role of bilateral investment agreements (BITs) that are not only to give guarantees for FDI but also allow a host country to regulate entry, impose conditions and specify performance requirements to ensure inward FDI's contribution to economic and social development, as well as environmental protection.

2.5 Summary

FDI research is based on integrative theories, such as international capital market theory, the firm theory, and the theory of international trade, which capture the FDI variables, namely ownership advantage, location advantage and internalisation of operations (OLI), termed as the Dunning's eclectic paradigm. Those eclectic and OLI-conscious FDI theories are, however, insufficient in fully explaining the direction of movement of FDI, as they conceptualised it to be mainly from the developed to the developing countries. That framing does not cater for the evolving trend of movements of FDI also from densely populated and land-scarce developing nations, such as India, to other developing countries, such as the African countries which have ample 'arable' land.

While large-scale agricultural investments that have been practised by industrialists from the West since about a century and half ago aimed to produce tropical industrial products, the new trend of agricultural investment since the mid-2000s is to produce basic food (such as wheat, rice, corn and soybeans) and biofuels to be exported to the investing country. Sources show that, since the mid-2000s, millions of hectares of virgin lands have been allocated for foreign investors in many African countries such as Ethiopia, Ghana, Madagascar and Mali. Issues regarding these huge agricultural land deals, have attracted research interest from scholars and have become advocacy issues by environmental and social activists. Theories that provide on those current developments and the determinants of FDI in large-scale agriculture are worthwhile.

3   FDI and agriculture

3.1 Introduction

Since the 1990s, the integration of developing countries in the global economy has increased mainly due to changing economic policies and the lowering of barriers to trade and investment (Athukorala, 2003). Between 1990 and 2007, the FDI inflows in the agricultural sector in SSA have significantly increased (see Figure 3.1) due to the food import needs of populous emerging markets, growing demand for biofuel production, and land and water shortages in investor countries (UNCTAD, 2009). Investor countries include Saudi Arabia, the United Arab Emirates, Qatar, Bahrain, the UK, Sweden, Denmark, Germany, China, South Korea, India, Malaysia, Singapore, Libya, Egypt, Djibouti and South Africa (Cotula, 2012; Brown, 2013).

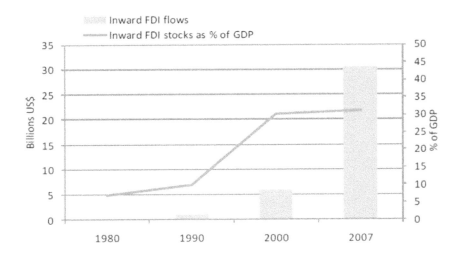

Figure 3.1 Foreign Investment Flows and Stocks in SSA
Source: Cotula et al. (2009, p. 25).

The 2007 and 2008 global food and financial crises that raised the price of agricultural products tremendously led countries that import food to focus on food production through investing in agricultural land abroad. These countries' tactics are to secure food for the long term so as to be less dependent on the volatility of global food prices. The global financial crisis, which led to a collapse in equity and bond markets, strengthened the competitiveness of FDI in agricultural land due to the anticipated profits from agricultural commodities (Görgen et al., 2009; Gerlach and Liu, 2010). Economic and financial crises have changed the FDI setting – that is investment in developing countries, mainly those in Africa, with arable land and usable water resources (Görgen et al., 2009). These changes in the global environmental and economic situation have begun to impact Africa's land resources in new and significant ways. The demand for energy and the rapid increase in FDI in agricultural land in Africa are the most noticeable reactions to these changes (Görgen et al., 2009).

3.2 Agricultural transformation strategies

Timmer (1988), Todaro (2000), Tsakok (2011), Lobao and Meyer (2001) and Ekonomifakta (2013) argue that the process of agricultural transformation starts when agricultural productivity per worker increases which, in turn, creates a surplus that can be utilised to develop the non-agricultural sector. As such, different strategies and farming techniques[1] were used to enable agricultural transformation in areas such as North America, Western Europe and Japan. The strategies include investing in transportation and communication infrastructure in order to expand market access for agricultural products and services and to sustain its development, expanding transportation and communication infrastructure development companies to absorb the excess farm labour force and locating labour-intensive light industries in rural areas to create employment and income to the excess farm labour force. The authors highlight the importance of knowing the stages and period over which agricultural transformation takes place. For instance, in Western Europe, Japan and North America, the agricultural transformation started from subsistence to diversified family agriculture to specialised commercial farming. This process took more than a century.

Dorward et al. (2003) and Jenkin (2011) have a similar view in the three phases of the agricultural development process leading to agricultural transformation. The authors emphasise the critical role of government in creating a conducive environment for transformation, such as the provision of effective agricultural research and extension programmes, as well as economic and social infrastructures. Dorward et al. (2003) further show evidence from India, where the government invested in fertiliser subsidies, roads and agricultural research and granted credit subsidies that led to high agricultural growth and poverty reduction. This confirms the importance of strictly adhering to the policy phases, which are establishing the basics, kick-starting markets and withdrawal. The authors criticise the current conventional policy in most SSA countries that attempt to move straight from phase 1 (i.e. establishing the basics such as roads, irrigation systems, research and land reforms) to phase 3, where the government withdraws for effective private-sector markets, which leads to a large volume of finance and input demand, produces supply and creates non-agricultural growth linkages. The government intervention (i.e. transaction cost subsidies) in phase 2 is overlooked. This encompasses seasonal finance, input supply systems and reliable local output markets which are critical for agricultural transformation.

Timmer (1988), Todaro (2000) and Ekonomifakta (2013) stress the advantage of agricultural transformation in economic development such as increasing the supply of food for domestic consumption and higher rural incomes; releasing the surplus of labour for industrial employment; expanding the size of the market for industrial output; increasing the supply of domestic savings; and earning in foreign exchange. This argument is, however, challenged by the empirical findings of Lobao et al. (2008) that reveal the negative impacts of large-scale agriculture on community well-being if it is not regulated and strictly monitored by the government. In the context of Ethiopia, it has formulated and adopted a number of economic and social policies and strategies, such as agricultural development–led industrialisation (ADLI), to facilitate agricultural transformation (see Section 6.2).

3.3 Investors in large-scale agriculture and target countries

Tran-Nguyen (2010) found that cash-poor low-income countries with arable land and usable water resources are the targets of foreign investors. Other studies distinguish the target countries as developing countries with low global market integration and export-oriented developing countries with established access to world markets (UNCTAD, 2009; FAO, 2009). The countries in Africa where investments take place include Ethiopia, Ghana, Sudan, Mozambique, Mali, Madagascar, Sierra Leone, Democratic Republic of Congo, Cameroon, Zambia, Angola, Tanzania and Benin. The countries in Asia most associated with FDI are Cambodia, the Philippines, Indonesia and Laos. Latin American FDI host countries are Argentina, Colombia, Brazil and Bolivia. In Europe, Russia and Ukraine are FDI hosts (Cuffaro and Hallam, 2011; Metcalfe and Kepe, 2008; Cotula and Vermeulen, 2009; Hallam, 2009; UNCTAD, 2009; FAO, 2009; Tran-Nguyen, 2010).

The FDI in agricultural land is handled by private and state-owned companies originated from different countries such as the US, the UK, Sweden, China, the Arab Gulf states (Saudi Arabia, Kuwait, Qatar and the United Arab Emirates), Libya, Egypt, India, Japan and South Korea (see Figure 3.2; UNCTAD, 2009). This map covers only confirmed deals that have been signed and some of which are implemented as of 2014.

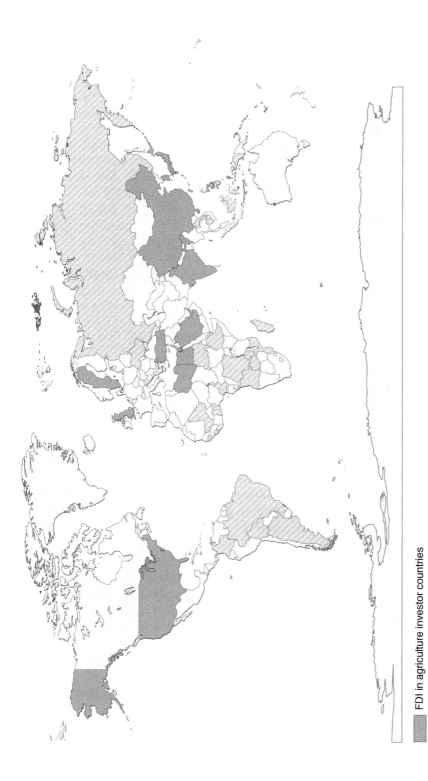

FDI in agriculture investor countries

FDI in agriculture target countries

Figure 3.2 Investors and Target Regions/Countries in Agricultural Land Investment Between 2006–2014

3.4 Drivers of FDI in large-scale agriculture

Various studies indicate the main drivers of inward FDI in large-scale agriculture to be of economic and political/strategic nature. The economic drivers include reducing import costs for food, increasing shareholder value because of rising food prices and emerging agro-fuel markets, securing future energy and food needs and anticipating growing land prices. The political and strategic drivers include meeting growing demand for food and agro-fuels, complying with international agreements such as the Kyoto protocol and reducing the dependency on the world market for food and fuel (Gerlach and Liu, 2010; Global Policy Forum, 2012; Tran-Nguyen, 2010; Hallam, 2009; Ndikumana and Verick, 2007).

Furthermore, these studies reveal that the majority of FDI in land in low-income countries serves to secure food and energy for growing populations in the investing countries. Food security is found to be the main driver for (cash-rich) investing countries such as the Arab Gulf states, which cannot produce enough crops to feed their population as they have critical water scarcity. In these countries, for instance, food price inflation has been a serious issue as it drives inflation in the wider economy (Tran-Nguyen, 2010). By 2030, the population of Gulf states is predicted to be about 60 million compared to 30 million in 2000, thus exacerbating this driver of FDI in the future (Cotula and Vermeulen, 2009).

3.5 Social, economic and environmental impacts of FDI in agriculture

De Schutter (2009) states that more FDI in rural areas of SSA can be particularly effective in reducing poverty, where it is concentrated. Liu (2004) further confirms the importance of agricultural investment in developing countries to ensure food and nutrition security and reducing poverty. Hallam (2009) reaffirms the narrative on the potential benefits from FDI in agricultural lands, such as an increase in employment of the local people through contract farming or joint ventures with local communities. The author, however, reveals that the foreign investors in agricultural land fully own and control the projects. This is further confirmed by Tran-Nguyen (2010), who reveals that foreign investors often bring workers from home. Second, these kinds of projects are generally capital-intensive, and thus, they do not generate much employment for the local smallholder farmers or landless peasants. Görgen et al. (2009) stress that these negative social impacts of FDI in agriculture may lead to social tensions and increase urban poverty as the unemployed local farmers could immigrate to urban areas to look for work or to generate income. It can also lead to a loss of traditional cultural practices.

Many scholars argue that environmental sustainability in agricultural production is a major issue in the context of large-scale FDI in agricultural land. Intensive agricultural production has a huge negative impact on biodiversity, forest, land, soil and water resources. These adverse impacts, in turn, adversely affect the well-being of the local community (Görgen et al., 2009; De Schutter, 2011; Masaba et al., 2013; Lobao et al., 2008; Hallam, 2009; Williams, 2012).

Görgen et al. (2009) and Hallam (2009) suggest the use of environmentally friendly production methods, an increase in the quality standard for food production and a reduction of erosion by producing in formerly abandoned land and enhancing afforestation to pre-empt the negative impacts of large-scale agriculture on the environment.

The study of Lobao et al. (2008) in 50 communities concludes that remote rural communities need a high level of government protection from the adverse impacts of commercial farming as the local government is weak to ensure the protection of local community's well-being.

3.6 Domestic law and agricultural investment contracts

A large number of scholars state that land tenure rights, water rights, environmental law, labour law on farms and other regulations in the agricultural sector are inadequate or non-existent in many developing countries (De Schutter, 2011; Masaba et al., 2013; Lobao et al., 2008; Williams, 2012; Tran-Nguyen, 2010). Hallam (2009), and Tran-Nguyen (2010) show that the domestic law often lacks comprehensiveness and clarity, especially in protecting the interests of the local community, such as smallholder farmers and poor rural dwellers.

Hallam (2009) and Tran-Nguyen (2010) both stress that the legal framework, including agricultural investment contracts and agreements that are signed by both foreign investors and host governments, protect foreign investor interests rather than local community interests. They speculate that investment contracts are most probably designed by individual investor countries and firms and thereby indirectly change or ignore the domestic law in host countries. This claim is further substantiated by Görgen et al. (2009) who reveal that the investment rules, especially BITs, often serve investor interests over local community interests. Tran-Nguyen (2010) emphasises that the legal implications of international investment contracts and treaties may restrict the government of a host country from taking measures to promote and protect rural communities and the natural environment.

3.7 Features of pro-poor and environmentally sustainable FDI in large-scale agriculture

Kakwani and Pernia (2000) and Grimm et al. (2007) argue that a development is pro-poor when its strategy is intentionally biased in favour of the poor so that the poor benefit proportionally more than the rich as opposed to trickle-down development.[2] The authors stress that growth is pro-poor when it absorbs labour and accelerates income growth among the poor.

De Schutter (2009), as well as Gordon and Pohl (2010), proposes a minimum set of core principles and measures for host states and investors in order to foster pro-poor and sustainable FDI in agricultural land. Görgen et al. (2009) identify economic, social-cultural and environmental factors as key indicators to measure sustainability and pro-poor investments. Similarly, several other studies conclude that participatory land-use planning (PLUP) and environmental impact assessment (EIA) as effective tools to ensure environmental, economic and social sustainability (FAO, 1993a; Kikula et al., 1993; FAO, 1995; Lohani et al., 1997; UNEP, 2004; EC, 2006; De Wit and Verheye, 2009; GIZ, 2012).

Gordon and Pohl (2010) emphasise that promoting sustainable and pro-poor investment in agricultural land requires addressing issues such as core labour standards, resettlement of local populations, public-sector transparency and environmental protection. That study also stressed the complex interconnections between the public sector and investor responsibilities in this area – "reaping the full benefits of investment in agriculture involves responsible behaviour by both government and investors and effective coordination between the two" (Gordon and Pohl, 2010, p. 4).

Lyakurwa (2009) and Djurfeldt (2012) argue that pro-poor and sustainable agricultural investment can only be realised if the essential elements are in place. The elements include good governance that prioritises poverty reduction, human development, productive employment, social integration and environmental protection. Lyakurwa (2009) and Djurfeldt (2012) further stress the active participation of poor households as labourers, producers and service providers to attain pro-poor and sustainable agriculture and rural development. They also stress that pro-poor agricultural growth strategies identify the importance of staple versus non-staple crops, the role of the state and the level of market integration (i.e. national and global).

Briassoulis (2004) reveals that intergovernmental collaboration is dependent on a favourable administrative culture (i.e. open, participatory) and an absence of intra-governmental power relations. Meijers and Stead (2004), Majumdar (2006) and Thabrew et al. (2009) further stress that intergovernmental coordination ensures consistency, coherence and comprehensiveness of the policies and practices of various sectors.

Masaba et al. (2013) highlight that pro-poor and sustainable FDI in agricultural land address the needs of smallholder farmers and rural communities, as well as improving their livelihoods and tenure security. The authors stress that pro-poor and sustainable FDI puts in place mechanisms in which implementation of investment agreements are monitored regularly in order to ensure the anticipated benefits for local community are realised, as well as to assess the impact of investments on rural development. The authors argue that the business arrangement made between rural community and foreign investors is a determining factor to ensure the agricultural investment is pro-poor and sustainable. They conclude that an inclusive business model is required for pro-poor and sustainable agriculture and rural development (Masaba et al., 2013).

Many scholars reveal the significant importance of community participation in decision-making to ensure the FDI in large-scale agriculture is pro-poor and environmentally sustainable (Storey, 1999; Lyakurwa, 2009; Curry, 1993; Persson, 2009; Warner, 1999; Yen and Luong, 2008; Irvin and Stansbury, 2004; Eguren,

2008; Masaba et al., 2013; Buccus et al., 2008). Storey (1999) and Curry (1993) argue that policies and programmes which regard the uniqueness of local social structure, economy, environment and culture are necessary but are not sufficient for successful policy and programme implementation without community playing a role in policy and programme formulation. Storey (1999), Majumdar (2006), Meijers and Stead (2004), Briassoulis (2004) and Thabrew et al. (2009) stress that intergovernmental coordination ensures consistency, coherence and comprehensiveness of various sectors' policies and practices.

3.8 Fundamental principles to promote pro-poor and environmentally sustainable FDI in large-scale agriculture

The minimum set of core principles and measures to advance environmentally sustainable and pro-poor FDI in large-scale agriculture, proposed by De Schutter (2009), are relevant to this book's focus (i.e. pro-poor and environmentally sustainable agricultural investments). These core principles, modified to suit the objectives of this book, include the human right to food, the land-use rights of indigenous people, the human rights of agricultural workers and the rights of local people to participate in the negotiation of large-scale agricultural land leases, as well as transparency and accountability in the use of revenues (see Table 3.1).

Gordon and Pohl (2010, p. 4) have a similar view of the fundamental principles for promoting pro-poor and sustainable investment in agriculture. Those principles are land and resource rights, food security, social and environmental sustainability, consultation and participation, economic viability, transparency, good governance and enabling environment. Along the same line, Görgen et al. (2009) have proposed measures for sustainability and pro-poor agricultural investment, such as economic, social and environmental effects of FDI. The impacts of these variables are presented in Table 3.2.

Table 3.1 Core Principles and Measures to Advance Pro-Poor and sustainable FDI in Large-Scale Agriculture

Core principles	Measures to advance pro-poor and sustainable FDI
The human right to food	Host states should ensure the provision of access to productive land for the local population when leasing or selling land to investors. They should ensure food security for the local population through investment revenues which will, in turn, be used to procure food in volumes equivalent to those which are produced for exports. They should ensure that a certain percentage of the crops produced shall be sold in the local market.

(Continued)

Table 3.1 (Continued)

Core principles	Measures to advance pro-poor and sustainable FDI
	Host state and investor should agree on certain conditions, such as farming system and wages, based on which the investment should be made. This would ensure that the investment agreement is geared at contributing fully to the local livelihoods through providing access to labour opportunities and a living wage for the local people involved in the FDI.
	Host states and investor should ensure that the modes of agricultural production shall respect the environment and therefore investors should adhere to high environmental standards in their activities. This would promote sustainable agricultural practices and sustainable forest management which contribute to safeguarding the environment as there is a strong link between the state of the environment and food production.
The land use rights of indigenous people	Host state should ensure individual or collective registration in favour of local communities to secure all their land use and other land rights. This would guarantee that their citizen's land could only be leased or sold to investors with their free, prior and informed consent and that they could be fully involved in future negotiations with potential investors. This would also protect the relationship between local communities and the land. In particular, indigenous people's distinct spiritual relationship with their land could be protected from forced removal and loss of other historical and traditional land rights.
The human rights of agricultural workers	The host state and investor should protect the fundamental human rights of agricultural workers. Specific labour rights such as working time, overtime pay, leave and wages should be specified. The occupational health and safety standards in agriculture should be regulated and enforced.
The rights of local people to participate in the negotiation of large-scale agricultural land leases	The right to self-determination and the exploitation of natural resources impose on host governments an obligation to protect individuals under their jurisdiction from being deprived of their access to productive resources due to the arrival of investors.
	The right to development – transparency and accountability in the use of revenues – requires host governments to ensure the adequate participation of the local communities concerned by land leases and that the decision-making process is fully transparent in order to ensure the long-term sustainability and success of investments. In addition, the right to development implies that FDI should contribute to local and national development in a responsible manner – i.e. social development, protection of the environment and respect the rule of law and fiscal obligations in the host countries.

Source: De Schutter (2009, modified).

Table 3.2 Positive and Negative Impacts of FDI in Agricultural Land

Relevant areas of FDI impacts	Positive Impact	Negative Impact
Economic	• Increasing productivity on agricultural land due to (a) better access to agricultural inputs such as seeds, fertiliser and capital; (b) applying technologies that raise yields and reduce postharvest losses; and (c) educating employees and farmers • Generating income by leasehold • Generating tax income by levy land taxes and increased employment • Improving infrastructure – i.e. building roads, investing in transportation and communication • Increasing agricultural exports due to increasing overall productivity and product quality • Transferring know-how and integrating the local economy into added value chains	• Reduced food security in the target country when food crops are not available for local consumption – i.e. export or replacement with industrial crops • Biased distribution of benefits in favour of the investor or just some sectors of the local population, not alleviating poverty but fuelling social conflicts • Competition in land use for food, animal feed and agrofuels with the poor suffering from high prices for land and water resources • Increase of local and regional unemployment when applying capital-intensive mechanisation or importing labour from investor country • In water-scarce areas, water availability for local farmers will reduce immensely
Social-cultural	• Improving living conditions and sustainable development by additional income possibilities in rural areas • Reactivation of abandoned land and value adding of underutilised land lead to income generation in rural areas • An increase in labour standards including wages, working hours, health insurance and other benefits • Better integration of local smallholder/family farmers • An increase in civil safety and political stability due to improved living conditions and a better integration of local small-size farmers	• A strong competition for remaining land can invoke land conflicts, leading to civil and political instability • Reducing access to land and marginalisation of small-size landowners has negative effects on any development geared towards the needs of the poor • Reduced access to land can lead to the displacement of indigenous people or exclusion of rural communities and increase rural poverty, especially for women who are involved in crop production • Emigration of local farmers can increase social tensions and urban poverty • A loss of inherent cultural habit may occur • Immigration of foreign employers can invoke social tension • Cultural and lingual divergences can also worsen social systems
Environmental	• An increase in environmentally friendly production methods can take place if foreign investors import practices that are more sustainable compared to local ones due to a higher level of education and better technical capacities • A reduction of erosion can be invoked by producing on formerly abandoned land • Training local farmers in environmentally sound production can strengthen awareness for the underlying problems and it can have spillover effects for other farms and lead as a kick-off for comprehensive natural resource management	• Increase in erosion and worsen climate change by displacing forest areas and other land use changes, which result in high carbon stock releases • A loss in water availability and quality due to large-scale water use and use of pesticides and fertiliser • A loss in soil quality due to an unsustainable use of chemicals • A reduction of biodiversity may be caused by large-scale monoculture production systems • Disruption of the local ecologic systems by introducing plants or species that are not part of the local biodiversity

Source: Görgen et al. (2009, pp. 21–24, modified).

3.9 Frameworks and guidelines to assess investment policies

There are global and regional frameworks and guidelines developed to serve as base materials in the formulation and implementation of national investment, policies, strategies, laws, rules and programmes for pro-poor and environmentally sustainable investment in large-scale agriculture and for effective agricultural sector development at large. These frameworks include the FAO voluntary guidelines on the responsible governance of tenure (FAO, 2012), the AUC–AfDB–UNECA Joint Land Policy Initiative's framework and guidelines (F&G) on land policy in Africa (AUC–AfDB–UNECA, 2010), and guidelines for agricultural contracts (FAO, 2001, 2004). The following subsections present these frameworks.

3.9.1 Global frameworks and guidelines

The global frameworks and guidelines on the responsible agricultural investment, endorsed by the Committee on World Food Security at its 38th session on 11 May 2012, address human rights and tenure rights through the provision of guidance to improve the governance of land tenure and other natural resources so as to achieve food security for all. The guidelines also encourage the achievement of the right to adequate food in the context of national food security, poverty eradication, sustainable livelihoods, social stability, rural development, environmental protection and sustainable social and economic development (FAO, 2012).

The guidelines spell out the responsibilities of host country governments and foreign investors to recognise and respect human rights and legitimate natural resources tenure rights. The guidelines suggest that host country government should provide and maintain policy, legal and institutional frameworks that advance responsible governance of land and other natural resources tenure. The guidelines stress the adherence to the overarching principles to promote responsible governance of land tenure. The principles include human dignity, non-discrimination, equity and justice, gender equality, holistic and sustainable approach, consultation and participation, rule of law, transparency, accountability and continuous improvement (FAO, 2012).

The FAO Good Practice Guidelines for Agricultural Leasing Arrangements (FAO, 2001, 2004) spells out the generic elements of a tenancy agreement. These include names of the parties, date of commencement, duration of the agreement, description of the property, rent, tenant's right to possession during the lease, use rights and responsibilities, upkeep of the land, condition of the land on return, arrangements for compensation, responsibility for paying taxes and other charges, the dispute resolution procedure and a record of the agreement (FAO, 2001, 2004). The Drake University Agricultural Law Centre's Landowner's Guide to Sustainable Farming (Cox, 2010) explains the key considerations for a sustainable farm lease agreement. The agreement includes tenure security, reimbursement for improvements, cost-sharing, risk-sharing, conservation provision and communication and ecosystem services (Cox, 2010).

3.9.2 Regional framework and guidelines

The AUC–AfDB–UNECA F&G on Land Policy in Africa (AUC–AfDB–UNECA, 2010) was endorsed by the AU member states in 2009 through an AU Declaration on Land Issues and Challenges in Africa (AU Assembly, July 2009). It is designed to assist African policy and decision-makers, practitioners and others in crafting efficient national land policies and programmes. The F&G stresses that land in Africa is a fundamental social and cultural asset, as well as a critically important development resource, especially for the poor. It is, therefore, paramount to have a land policy that balances the rights and interests of all users and ensures the inclusion of all members of society. In particular, women, persons with disability and other landless poor should be included to enable them to realise full social, environmental and economic benefits from land which, in addition, enhances political stability and democratic institution building. Adequate land policy provides broader ranging prescriptions for the management of cross-cutting issues such as those advancing environmental sustainability and poverty reduction (AU Assembly, July 2009).

This F&G further stresses the emerging global strategic land-related issues that have significant impacts on Africa's land resources. These issues include changes in the global ecosystem, demand for energy supplies and rapid increase in FDI. To prevent the negative consequences of these emerging issues and to lead to pro-poor and sustainable FDI in agricultural land, the F&G urges host countries to put in place adequate policies to ensure the risks associated with these investments, in particular the risk of uncompensated loss of land rights by the poor, are avoided or effectively managed. For the majority of African societies, land is considered as a social, cultural and ontological resource. Land policy development needs to address the social and cultural context of land, such as land and spirituality, if the objectives of the land policy are to be effectively implemented. The F&G urges African countries to ensure that financial and human resources are set aside to implement their land policy and other related policies, as well as to balance pro-poor priorities with market orientation (AUC-AfDB-UNECA, 2010).

The African Union Declaration on Land Issues and Challenges in Africa commits heads of states and governments of the African Union (AU) to reaffirm the commitments they have made to poverty eradication. The declaration further commits the AU member states to recognise the centrality of land to sustainable socio-economic growth, development and the security of the social, economic and cultural livelihoods of the African people. It reaffirms their awareness of the rich heritage of Africa's land and related resources especially its unique natural eco-systems. It also reaffirms their cognisance of the need for strong systems of land governance based on the principles of sustainability to ensure preservation, protection and renewability of Africa's land and related resources (AU Assembly, July 2009).

The African governments also commit to review their land sectors with a view to developing comprehensive policies that take into account their particular needs and to build adequate human, financial and technical capacities to support land policy development and implementation. The African leaders recognise the need to develop strong systems of land governance that understand the diversity and complexity of the systems under which land and land-based resources are held, managed and used (AU Assembly, July 2009).

AUC–AfDB–UNECA Guiding Principles on Large-Scale Land-Based Investments in Africa (AUC–AfDB–UNECA, 2014) urges that the contracts entered into by government and communities with investors should identify the rights and obligations of all parties. It recommends that the identified rights and obligations should be formulated in specific and enforceable terms in order to facilitate compliance monitoring and sanctioning non-compliance (AUC–AfDB–UNECA, 2014).

3.9.3 National frameworks and guidelines

The global and regional investment frameworks and guidelines (FAO, 2012; AU Assembly, July 2009; FAO, 2001, 2004; Cox, 2010; Land for Good Organization, 2012; AUC–AfDB–UNECA, 2014) are vital for development and assessment of national investment policy's contents and agricultural land lease agreement terms and conditions. For example, the Landowner's Guide to Leasing Land for Farming recommends that a lease agreement should include clauses on insurance and liability, monitoring and reporting and security deposit (Land for Good Organization, 2012; see Section 6.4).

In addition, empirical findings of agricultural transformation processes are also relevant to further assess the national investment policy with regard to pro-poor and environmentally sustainable agricultural development (see Sections 3.2 and 3.6).

3.10 Summary

Evidence shows that FDI inflows in the agricultural sectors in SSA have tremendously increased in the past recent years. It is mainly because the 2007 and 2008 global food and financial crises that considerably raised the prices of food and other agricultural products, such as biofuel, led investors to focus on agricultural production through investing in agricultural land abroad, thereby changing the magnitude and direction of movement of FDI. The investors in agricultural land are private and state-owned companies from different countries such as the UK, Sweden, China, the Arab Gulf states (Saudi Arabia, Kuwait, Qatar and the United Arab Emirates), Libya, Egypt, India, Japan and South Korea. The countries wherein investments take place include Ethiopia, Ghana, Sudan, Mozambique, Mali, Madagascar, Sierra Leone, Democratic Republic of Congo, Cameroon, Zambia, Angola, Tanzania and Benin in Africa; Cambodia, the Philippines, Indonesia and Laos in Asia; Argentina, Colombia, Brazil and Bolivia in Latin America; and Russia and Ukraine in Europe.

For investment in large-scale agriculture to be beneficial to the host country, it has to meet the minimum set of core principles and measures which include economic viability, pro-poorness (absorb labour and accelerate income growth among the poor) and environmental sustainability. PLUP and EIA, which signify good governance, are effective tools for ensuring environmental, economic and social sustainability. There are global, regional and national frameworks and guidelines that help to ensure socially and environmentally responsible large-scale agricultural investments, which, in turn, contributes to effective agricultural sector development.

Notes

1 The farming techniques applied include biologica-chemical (i.e. hybrid seeds, fertilisers and pesticides) and mechanical innovations.
2 Trickle-down development implies a vertical flow from the rich to the poor (i.e. the benefits of economic growth go to the rich first, and then the poor indirectly gain the benefits when the rich spend their gains; Kakwani and Pernia, 2000).

4 Research methodology

4.1 Introduction

In Chapter 1, a brief research methodology was presented. This chapter discusses in detail and justifies the research methodology applied in this book. The identified information gap on FDI in large-scale agriculture in Ethiopia begs for an in-depth study in the extent, nature and impact of these investments in Ethiopia. Robson (1993) argues that case study research gives an in-depth investigation of entities that look for further theoretical understanding and practical knowledge of a real-world phenomenon. Yin (2003) further argues that case study methodology enables to conduct research that requires an empirical investigation of a specific event within its real-life context using multiple sources of evidence. The appropriateness of case study methodology for research related to agriculture and FDI are further confirmed by AUC–AfDB–UNECA Joint Land Policy Initiative's (2011) concept note for the high-level policy forum on "Land Based FDI in Africa: Making Investment Work for African Agricultural Development" and Hough and Neuland (2000) study on "Global Business Environments and Strategies: Managing for Global Competitive Advantage".

FDI in large-scale agriculture is a complex issue that involves economic, social, political, environmental and cultural aspects. It requires multifaceted methodology rich in contextual analysis. It needs to be examined and analyzed in its specific environment of occurrence. Hence, this book identifies case study methodology to be the appropriate research method that enables conducting an in-depth empirical investigation so as to provide detailed data on the extent, nature and impacts of these investments in Ethiopian as the existing studies on this issue lack sufficient details to determine whether these investments are economically, socially and environmentally viable or not. Chapter 7 presents the description of the case study projects of this book.

The research questions of this book are contemporary, specific and critical involving many people with different interest. The primary people include Ethiopian government, foreign investors and local communities. The chosen methodology is compatible with critical realism paradigm, which is the philosophical grounding of this book, and has been used to good effect in this combination by Whittal (2008) and Mabesa and Whittal (2011). Section 4.2 provides a brief description of Ethiopia's ethnic-based federalism system to substantiate further the appropriateness of case study methodology for this book.

Case study methodology has been criticised in requiring more time and money to produce scientific results. Its product can be detailed and lengthy which may be unsuitable to busy policy makers and practitioners as it requires a great deal of time to read, understand and use (Stake, 2005). The final product could be influenced by the author's biases (Guba and Lincoln, 1981). A case study may have limitations of reliability, validity and generalisability if it lacks representativeness and rigour in the collection, construction and analysis of the empirical data (Hamel, 1993). This book conducts multiple case studies, which are often regarded as reliable and increases the robustness of the study (see Section 4.3). This book is cognisant of conducting multiple cases may require more resources and time compared to a single case study, and it identifies different ways to secure the required resources.

This book admits the difficulties of reporting from an objective standpoint. Hence, this book applies critical thinking skills that enable the author to remove personal bias and methodically evaluate each case. The primary target audiences of these book findings are Ethiopian policy makers and policy implementers at all levels of government (federal, regional, district, and kebele) followed by foreign investors, local community representatives, development partners such as UN entities and bilateral and multilateral donors, as well as the public who are interested in this matter. The author of this book is aware of these diverse audiences and prepared the analysis of this study to cater for this variety of readers.

4.2 Ethiopian federal system

Aalen (2002, p. 20), and Teshome and Záhořík (2008, p. 2) articulate the pure meaning of federalism as a "division of power" and a "decentralized government". These authors, however, stress that a country's economic, political and social conditions determine the federal system to be either symmetrical or asymmetrical. Aalen (2002) and Teshome and Záhořík (2008) further describe that the relationship of the vertical levels of government is largely determined by various social, economic and political conditions of a country. The introduction of ethnic federalism is one of the reforms Ethiopia introduced since the 1991 regime change. Accordingly, the Ethiopian state structure has a federal government at the centre and nine regional states pursuant to the transitional charter (Proclamation No.7/1992) and the subsequent 1995 Federal Constitution of Ethiopia (Proclamation No. 1/1995).

Ethiopian regions are very different from one another when it comes to the ethnic composition, size of population and area, economic development and political landscape. This implies that the regions have different capacities to implement the constitutional provisions. Also, the level of intervention by the central government varies in each region. For instance, regions such as Gambella and Beneshangul-Gumuz that are classified as emerging regions suffer from extreme poverty and have a serious lack of capacity to implement the decentralisation programme. As such, they depend on the central government's technical and financial assistance to administer their respective regions thus relinquishing their regional autonomy. The case study projects of this book are located in these two regions.

According to Aalen (2002), the Ethiopian federal government gets the largest share of the revenue of taxes compared to regions. The author concludes that this privilege gives the most lucrative income sources to the federal government. Berhanu (n.d.)[1] further elaborates on the Ethiopian federation and states that the incumbent party in power, the EPRDF, controls all branches of government both at the federal and state levels through the party system and its affiliates. Thus, the Ethiopian ethnically based federalist system is asymmetrical, and the lack of financial independence of the regions contributes to a weakening of the federal division of power (Aalen, 2002; Teshome and Záhořík, 2008).

4.3 Case and unit of analysis

The scope of this book is FDI in large-scale agriculture in Ethiopia to which the case study results are intended to be generalised. The choice of the cases (i.e. investment projects) is motivated by some of the following guiding factors:

a   The investment is a foreign investment.
b   The number of years the land has been leased, that is two years and more. This is because the investment directive for agricultural land states that once the land is leased, activity for which the land is leased should start within two years. This allows seeing whether the land is leased on speculation of the future increase in land price and whether the activity is in line with the agreed-on activity or a different one (e.g. rice production converted to biofuels).
c   The size of the land – more than 5,000 hectares. According to the regulation by the Council of Ministers on the administration of agricultural investment land under the appointment of regions, large arable lands mean farmlands exceeding the area of 5,000 hectares that the regional government transferred to the federal government to administer the land for agricultural development (Zenawi, 2010).
d   The type of agricultural activities (agricultural products), that is food crops or biofuel crops
e   The purpose of the investment – that is, is the product targeted for the domestic market or export?

The reason for items (d) and (e) in the preceding list is to see whether the agricultural products from these leased lands by foreigners has a possibility to contribute to Ethiopia's food security either directly through contribution or indirectly through increasing Ethiopia's foreign earnings to import the required foods.

There are nine regions and two administrative cities (Addis Ababa and Dire Dawa) in Ethiopia (see Figure 4.1). The FDI in the agricultural land more than 5,000 hectares is concentrated in only in three regions, namely Gambella, Beneshangul-Gumuz and Southern Nations, Nationalities, and Peoples' Region (SNNPR). There is therefore little choice in the case study areas, and all areas where the majority of FDI in large-scale agriculture are prevalent are included (see Table 4.1). There was one investment project in SNNPR during the case selection of the cases that fulfilled this book's case study selection criteria. However, this investment project was not operational during data collection for this book in December 2014. Hence, SNNPR is excluded from this study (see Table 4.2).

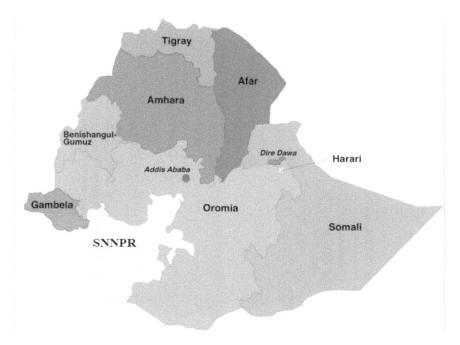

Figure 4.1 Administrative Map of Ethiopia
Source: WHO (2003).

Table 4.1 Regions Where FDI in Large-Scale Agriculture Exists in 2011

Region name	Number of FDI in large scale agriculture in 2011**	Name of investor company	Nationalities	Type of Investment	Total land Leased in hectare	Year of agreement signed
Beneshangul-**Gumuz**	2	CLC Industries PLC	Indian	Cotton	25,000	December 2009
		Shaporji (S&P) Energy Solutions PLC	Indian	Pongamia (bio-fuel tree)	50,000	March 2010
Gambella	7	Toren Agro Industries PLC	Turkey	Cotton & Soya bean	6,000	September 2011
		Ruchi Agri PLC	Indian	Soya bean	25,000	April 2010
		BHO Bio Products PLC	Indian	Edible oil crops	27,000	May 2010
		Sannati Agro Farm Enterprises PLC	Indian	Rice	10,000	October 2010
		Saudi Star Agricultural Development PLC	Saudi	Rice	10,000	September 2009
		Karuturi Agro Products PLC	Indian	Palm, cereals, rice & sugarcane	100,000	August 2008
		Sabre Farms PLC	Indian	Cotton & Soya bean	25,000	May 2011
SNNPR*	1	Whitefield Cotton Farm PLC	Indian	Cotton	10,000	August 2010

* Southern Nations, Nationalities, and People's Region.
** The cut-off year for this study is 2011 as agricultural development needs time to show results.

Table 4.2 Selected Case Study Regions and Foreign Large-Scale Agricultural Investments

Item no.	Region name	The # of case study projects	Name of investor company	Nationalities	Type of Investment	Total land leased in hectare	Year of agreement signed	Duration (years)**
1	Beneshangul-Gumuz	1	Shaporji (S&P) Energy Solutions PLC	Indian	Pongamia (biofuel tree)	50,000	March 2010	50
2	Gambella	5	Toren Agro Industries PLC	Turkey	Cotton & soya bean	6,000	September 2011	25
			Ruchi Agri PLC	Indian	Soya bean	25,000	April 2010	25
			BHO Bio Products PLC	Indian	Edible oil crops	27,000	May 2010	25
			Saudi Star Agricultural Development PLC	Saudi	Rice	10,000	September 2009*	50
			Karuturi Agro Products PLC	Indian	Palm, cereals, rice & sugarcane	100,000	August 2008*	50

* In 2010, the Council of Ministers passed a regulation on the administration of large-scale farmlands (i.e. more than 5,000 hectares) by the federal government. Regional governments transferred these lands to the federal government. Hence, Saudi Star Agricultural Development PLC and Karuturi Agro Products PLC, signed contracts in 2009 and 2008, respectively, with the Gambella regional government, had to re-sign a contract with the federal government in October 2010.

** The lease period is renewable for another term if the two parties agree.

4.4 Selection of the case study areas

Based on the established criteria (see Section 4.3), six foreign large-scale agricultural investment projects were identified for inclusion in this study. Five of them are located in Gambella Regional State, while one of them is situated in Beneshangul-Gumuz Regional State. These foreign investment projects leased a total of 218,000 hectares of land for cotton, soya bean, sugarcane, rice, palm and biofuel tree production (see Table 4.2). The multiple cases were used in this book so as to ensure the robustness of the conclusion of this study. This is substantiated by Yin (1994) who argues that multiple cases significantly provide analytic benefits as the analytic conclusions independently arising from two or more cases which are more powerful than coming from a single case alone.

FDI in large-scale agriculture on more than 5,000 hectares of land in Ethiopia are concentrated in three regions but mainly in Gambella as indicated in Table 4.1. Most of them (i.e. 6 out of 10 investment projects – in other words, two out of three regions) were included in this study, which is considered sufficient to generalise the findings to Ethiopia.

4.5 Data sources

Yin (2003) and Robson (1993) argue that multiple data sources provide evidence which enhances data validity and reliability. The authors identify and describe six methods of data collection in case study research. These methods are documentation, archival records, interviews, direct observation, participants' observation and physical artefacts. Ndikumana and Verick (2007) used multiple case studies in order to analyze the causes and effects of FDI in 38 SSA economies from 1970 to 2005. The data collection method of these case studies was documentation. Similarly, Gerlach and Liu (2010) applied multiple case studies to analyze the economic, social and environmental impacts of resource-seeking FDI on host countries in eight African countries. Görgen et al. (2009) also used documentation in multiple case studies to assess FDI in land in Cambodia, Laos, Madagascar and Mali. For this book, documentation, archival records, interviews and direct observations were used to examine the history of FDI in large-scale agriculture in Ethiopia, the current Ethiopian investment policy's support to FDI in large-scale agriculture, community's participation in the process of these investments in the selected investment projects' areas and the contribution of these investments to Ethiopia's economic growth, social development and environmental protection. This study made the required efforts to seek the cooperation of all informants as it was necessary to get the relevant documents for the study and responses to all key questions. The detail of these data collection methods is described in Sections 4.5.1 through 4.5.4. The data which were collected date between 1930 and 2016.

The procedure that was pursued in this book to collect data includes the following:

• Identification of government agencies where the relevant documents for this study were available. Also, each agency contact person and major informants' full name, position and address were sourced.

- A summary of the background information of the study, which included the statement of the problem and objective of the study and the rationale for selecting the study areas, together with an introductory letter were handed over to all agencies and individuals.
- During delivery of the letter, any relevant documents for the study were requested, and some were obtained. Tentative interview dates were arranged.

This book made efforts to corroborate the information gathered from interviews and focus group discussions with other sources of data since key informants provided evidence from only their perspective and bias needed to be considered. Hence, the author of this book looked at the same types of data from many other sources in order to validate the data's accuracy. These multiple sources of evidence led to a data source triangulation where the information obtained from key informants (see Section 4.5.3) was cross-verified so as to increase the credibility and validity of the data and hence the results. In addition, the cross-verified primary data were confirmed with the information obtained from the secondary data (see Sections 4.5.1 and 4.5.2) to further ensure its accuracy. As Yin (2003) claims, it is inevitable for a researcher to intrude into participants' territory when conducting case studies that involve interviews. This claim is confirmed by this book, which involved a range of participants during data collection and the author of this book had to intrude into the participants' territory to gather the information. Conversely, this book adhered to the case study protocol, including procedures and general rules, and ensured that approval is sought in advance of the data collection.

4.5.1 Documentation

The documentation that was gathered for this study derived from an array of sources including national policies, policy-based proclamations, long-term development plans, contractual agreements and reports from the imperial regime to the current government of Ethiopia (see Appendix 2). The documents from previous governments were used to assess the nature and history of FDI in agriculture in Ethiopia (see Chapter 5). These documents were assessed based on the established analytical frameworks and guidelines to assess investment policy that promotes environmentally sustainable and pro-poor investments (see Chapter 3). It is always difficult to getting access to documents in Ethiopia, especially issues like FDI in large-scale agriculture which is politically very sensitive as there have been criticisms from different groups. However, different ways, such as identifying and approaching people who have direct or indirect connections with officials in various government offices, were used to get access to the documents. Most of the key documents were obtained, except the environmental impact assessment reports of the two selected companies (see Appendix 2, Section 6). The list of documents can be found in Appendix 2.

4.5.2 Archival records

Archival records such as charts of the geographical characteristics or layouts of the study areas as well as survey data such as census records or data previously collected about the study areas were used. In addition, site plans of the case study agricultural investment projects were used. These documents were obtained from the following:

- Ethiopian Central Statistics Authority
- Gambella Regional State Statistics Bureau
- Gambella Regional State Wildlife Conservation Authority (National Park Office)
- Investment projects of Saudi Star, Karuturi, Toren and BHO

These archival records enabled to confirm or refute some of the data from interviews as well as studies with regard to previous utilisation of the investment projects' lands in Ethiopia (see Cotula and Vermeulen, 2009) "Deal or no deal: the outlook for agricultural land investment in Africa" and the Oakland Institute (2011) "Understanding land investment deals in Africa – Country report: Ethiopia").

4.5.3 Interviews

Interviews are major sources of case study evidence as most case studies involve human affairs (Yin, 2003; Robson, 1993). Open-ended interviews and focus group discussions were applied in this study. In an open-ended interview, the key respondents were asked questions related to their offices' mandates/functions in agricultural investments. Some of these interviewees became key informants and suggested other persons to be interviewed and provided other sources of evidence that were closely associated with the research questions. The key informants were critical to the success of this study. This study had three groups of key informants who have different interests. Those are government officials, investment company representatives and farm/factory workers and local residents (i.e. indigenous people) in the area of the investment projects. The total number of key informants in all the three groups was 144 (see Appendix 1).

The government officials who were interviewed in this book include the high-level government officials at the federal, regional, district and kebele[2] levels. At the federal level, officials such as directors-general, who have the mandate to authorise FDI in large-scale agriculture (i.e. more than 5,000 hectares) were included. At the regional level, officials such as heads of bureau, who are decision-makers for their respective region with regard to agricultural investments, were interviewed. At the district (*woreda*) level, officials such as district administrators and experts, who have a direct relationship with the agricultural projects' activities, especially in monitoring and evaluation, provided critical information. At the kebele level, the chairpersons of the kebeles were interviewed individually.

The other key informants of this book are the foreign agricultural investment projects' representatives or managers. These key informants are responsible for their respective company's involvement in the large-scale agricultural investment in Ethiopia. Interviews were only conducted with those who accepted the invitation for the interview. The author was also able to interview the farm and factory workers of these investment projects who provided vital information on the operation of the farms, as well as the factory, in terms of adherence to rules and regulations of labour and environment.

Focus group discussions with affected communities of the case studies projects areas were arranged in order to confirm the evidence gathered from other sources. The key informants of the focus group discussions were selected randomly and consisted of both genders, young and old. The discussions were conducted in a conversational manner but focusing on the main issues of FDI in large-scale agriculture processes and impacts on their localities. Questions were carefully worded in order to confirm or refute information gained from other data sources such as the local government, community elders and the investment projects representatives. Since each community has its own ethnic group and speaks its ethnic language, quite a number of interpreters and facilitators were used, a necessity for the focus group discussions with these communities. The community elders, who were recognised and respected and were involved in the arbitration of their community matters, were interviewed individually (see Appendix 1).

These interviews were conducted in English and Amharic (the working language of Ethiopia). A recording device was not used as it likely causes discomfort to the interviewee, and instead of recording, active listening technique was employed along with detailed interview note taking. These notes were the core interview data.

4.5.4 *Direct observation*

Direct observation is necessary to verify the data obtained from documents and interviews (Yin, 2003). The author undertook field visits to the case study areas to collect additional data, which largely consisted of interviews and direct observations. The author made tremendous efforts to enhance the reliability of the observational evidence. Hence, she took a research team consisting of a research assistant, technical assistants and interpreters, as well as district administrators and kebele chairmen. Each had different backgrounds and functions in order to complement and validate the data obtained from direct observation (see Appendix 3).

The purpose of the direct observation of the case study project areas is manifold. First, the direct observation enabled the author to ascertain if the foreign investors were using the leased lands for the agreed purposes. Second, if the foreign investor had developed the land and produced the agricultural products as per the agreed scheduled. Third, direct observation enabled the author to determine if these investments created employment for local people and improved the local living standards (i.e. better roads, schools and health centres). Fourth, the direct observation of the case study farms enabled the author to assess the environmental performance of the investment projects, including execution of the mitigation measures which are identified in the projects' EIA reports. Similarly, this study was able to assess the adherence of the investment projects to the Ethiopian Environmental Code of Practice for Agricultural Investment which spells out all the precautions measures to prevent environmental degradation due to the agricultural activities. In addition, the direct observation of the agricultural sites enabled the author to evaluate the adherence of the agricultural projects to the Ethiopian labour laws, especially occupational safety and health (see Appendix 3).

4.6 Research ethics and positioning

It is difficult to report from an objective standpoint the researcher's bias and qualities of research (Yin, 2003). Nonetheless, critical thinking skills enable researchers/analysts to remove personal bias and analytically or methodically evaluate a particular situation (Henley-Putnam University, 2011). This approach was taken in the course of this book. The author self-financed all her studies, including a BA (Public Administration and Business Management), an MSc (Environmental Management and Policy) and an MPH (Master of Public Health), as well as a PhD in Development Studies. All of these degree programmes were highly oriented towards social science with little natural science elements and founded in the post-positivism paradigm.

The author was born in Ethiopia. Prior to this book, the author published books on an environmental-related subject and had been involved in reviewing the various Ethiopian policies and strategies that are designed to reduce poverty and advance sustainable development. She is knowledgeable of the Ethiopian political, socio-economic, cultural and environmental conditions. In addition, the author has a good knowledge of other African countries' social, economic and political development. This background and experience have provided the author a unique, but essential, experience of the Ethiopian context and helped her tremendously to have a thorough understanding of the case studies – this would otherwise have been impossible.

The negative influence of bias on the study results and on the generalisability of the findings was controlled through multifaceted triangulation in the collection and analysing the case study data. The author's experience and expertise in soft systems methodologies and case study research facilitated the conducting of this study.

4.7 Analysis

The analysis of this book is based on the analytical frameworks that were established in Chapter 3, as well as the theoretical foundation (i.e. critical realism), discussed in Section 1.3.1. This book started by analysing the data as soon as the data collection started and continued after the data collection. This approach is in conformity with Yin (2003), who suggests that analysis of case study starts when data collection commences.

This author of this book first developed a matrix where the interview questions, derived from the research questions, were grouped. Responses from each interview question by the various key informants were placed within such groups. The grouping was done using a colour code. Each key informant who was asked the same questions were given similar colour code.

The primary questions of this book deal with the Ethiopian investment policy support to the FDI in large-scale agriculture, as well as the policy encouragement for pro-poor and environmentally sustainable FDI in large-scale agriculture in Ethiopia. The Ethiopian investment policy support to the FDI in large-scale agriculture was assessed in two parts. The first part was the policy contents which was assessed against the global and regional frameworks and guidelines that are developed to support the formulation and implementation of national investment strategies, policies, laws, rules and programmes for effective agricultural sector development (see Chapter 6). The second part was the investment policy implementation which was assessed using the six case studies of this book (see Chapter 7). These foreign large-scale agricultural investment projects (the case studies) were also used to assess the strength of the institutions that promote agricultural investments and facilitate the operation of these investments in order to make them productive and to achieve the investment policy objectives (see Sections 6.3 and 6.5). Further analysis was made using the empirical findings of previous studies on FDI and host country policies and best practices (see Chapter 2) to determine the Ethiopian investment policy support to FDI in large-scale agriculture.

In addition, the practical support of the Ethiopian investment policy for these foreign agricultural investments (the case studies) set up to promote pro-poor and environmentally sustainable FDI in large-scale agriculture was assessed against the framework to promote environmentally sustainable and pro-poor FDI in large-scale agriculture (see Section 3.9). Each case was assessed against the framework to determine as pro-poor and environmentally sustainable or not. The performance of each case study against each criterion for pro-poor and environmentally sustainable investment was assessed using a five-level rating system ranging from *very good* to *poor*. The numerical scores are assigned on a normative basis based on each case study's performance (see Table 8.1). Relevant findings of previous research were also used to deepen the analysis so as to conclude the practical support of the Ethiopian investment policy to FDI in large-scale agriculture to be pro-poor and environmentally sustainable while accelerating economic growth.

The cross-case analysis of the six agricultural projects in terms of their performance on the protection of the environment, contribution to social and economic development ascertain common conclusions on the support of the Ethiopian investment policy for pro-poor and environmentally sustainable FDI in large-scale agriculture (see Figure 8.1).

Furthermore, the historical background of FDI in large-scale agriculture in Ethiopia was reviewed to further enhance the understanding of the FDI trends and substantiate the conclusions on the nature and extent of the FDI in large-scale agriculture in Ethiopia (see Chapter 5).

4.8 Summary

A case study methodology is identified as appropriate for this book. This methodology is also compatible with a critical realist paradigm which is the theoretical framework of this study. Multiple case studies were undertaken. The selection criteria of the cases were established in accordance with the purpose of the book. This book included 70% of the cases of FDI in large-scale agriculture in Ethiopia in order to enhance the internal validity and the analytical generalisation to the theory on Ethiopian investment policy support to FDI in large-scale agriculture as well as the Ethiopia-rising narrative.

The selected case studies (i.e. agricultural projects) led to the case study areas. All three regions where FDI in large-scale agriculture is concentrated were selected. These regions are Gambella, Beneshangul-Gumuz and SNNPR. However, during data collection, the case study in SNNPR was not operational, and thus, it is excluded. Several data collection strategies were used, including documentation, in-depth interviews, focus group discussions and archival records, as well as direct observation. These various sources of data collection strategies were very useful and complementary. They enable data triangulation which enhances the validity of the research.

The analytical framework is that each case study is analyzed using tools identified as part of the research. These case-by-case results were cross-compared (cross-case analysis) in order to draw general conclusions on the Ethiopian investment policy support to pro-poor and environmentally sustainable FDI in large-scale agriculture in Ethiopia (see Chapters 7 and 8).

The next three chapters present the history and nature of FDI in agriculture in Ethiopia, current Ethiopian policies and institutions that facilitate FDI in large-scale agriculture including the agricultural land-lease format as well as case study narratives. Chapter 8 follows with the analysis and reflections of the case studies and their results in terms of economic, social and environmental sustainability. Chapter 9 concludes with implications.

Notes

1 N.d. – no date
2 A "kebele" is at the village level, is mandated to administer all local issues and is directly responsible for creating a viable environment for its community (i.e. protecting its community's culture, livelihoods and natural resources).

5 History and nature of FDI in Ethiopian agriculture

5.1 Introduction

It is imperative to understand the historical account of FDI in agriculture in Ethiopia in order to adequately analyze the current trend of FDI in agriculture. The purpose of this chapter is, therefore, to present the trends of FDI in agriculture in Ethiopia, which will shed light on the nature and magnitude of FDI. This will also provide a context in relation to Ethiopia's social and economic development milestones, as well as the effect on Ethiopia of global economic and political shifts. This chapter covers the FDI history from 1930 to date. This is because, before 1930, the Ethiopian Empire was administered on a regional basis by local chieftains and provincial aristocrats. It was Emperor Haile Selassie I who managed to consolidate the Empire under one unified administration and ruled the country from 1930 to 1974 (MoI, 1964a).

FDI in agriculture has therefore a long history in Ethiopia and was first practised during Emperor Haile Selassie I. The imperial regime was overthrown by a military coup in 1974. This military regime with communist ideology governed Ethiopia from 1974 to 1991. During this period, FDI was discouraged while state-owned large farms were promoted (see the Provisional Military Administration Council Proclamation of 1975 on government ownership and control of means of production as well as the Declaration on Economic Policy of Socialist Ethiopia, 1975). The current Ethiopian government, the EPRDF, has been in power since the overthrow of the military regime in 1991. The EPRDF quickly realised the failure of the military government's economic policy as well as recognising global political and economic shifts such as the end of the Cold War (Turner, 1993). Along with many African and Eastern European countries, it reformed the economic policy and adopted a market economy with the support of the Bretton Woods Institutions (Geda, 2006). The EPRDF government encourages FDI in agriculture, which is evident from its agricultural and rural development policies and strategies (MoFED, 2003).

All three regimes have acknowledged the importance of agriculture in the Ethiopian economy and advocated for agricultural sector development as the economic pillar of Ethiopia. However, the strategy applied to develop the sector varies between the military regime, which discouraged FDI in agriculture, and the imperial regime and the EPRDF government that encouraged FDI in large-scale agriculture and, in the case of the current EPRDF government, still does so. Against such a background, the subsections that follow present an in-depth analysis of these three ideologically different policies towards FDI in agriculture and reveal their similarities and differences.

In addition, analyses of the discussion on the contents of the current investment policy in relation to FDI in large-scale agriculture, as well as its implementation and the institutions that are mandated to implement the investment policy are presented in the next chapter.

5.2 FDI during the imperial regime: policies and practices

It was during the imperial regime that the modernisation of Ethiopia was envisaged through the expansion of modern schools, health facilities, formulation and adoption of the first Ethiopian constitution and various socio-economic policies, the beginning of medium-term planning, the development of infrastructure (such as road and air transportation, electric and thermal power, telecommunications, postal services, banking, ports and shipping)[1] and the construction of modern buildings (MoI, 1973; Henze, 2000; Geda, 2006; Kefale, 2009). This regime recognised the importance of agriculture in the Ethiopian economy and the role it would play for a long time to come. As such, the imperial regime focused on establishing major agricultural institutions, such as the Alemaya College of Agricultural Engineering and Mechanical Arts, the Agricultural Experimental Station and a number of community development centres, so as to scale up the scientific development of agriculture in Ethiopia. The regime also recognised small family farms, prevalent in Ethiopia, even though their productivity was very low due to the underdevelopment of the methods used to produce agricultural products. Hence, the government encouraged the establishment of foreign-owned large-scale commercial farms to modernise and transform the agricultural sector while supporting small family farms to increase productivity (MoI, 1964b; Henze, 2000). FDI was also encouraged to increase foreign resources, which were needed to import capital goods (IEG, 1962).

The regime faced several crises: the Italian Fascist occupation of Ethiopia (1935–41), the Great Depression[2] of the 1930s, the World War II (1939–45) and the Cold War (1947–91). These all had significant implications on the political stability, as well as the socio-economic development, of Ethiopia (Klapsis, 2014). These global political and economic crises, especially the Great Depression and the Italian fascist occupation, had a bearing on the direction of Ethiopia's strategic development. Hence, the enactment of Ethiopia's development policies and programmes started after 1941. The focus was on specific sectors like agriculture, infrastructure[3] and social transformation[4] in order to bring the desired development goals (MoI, 1941; Essays-UK, 2013).

During this government, three five-year plans[5] were developed with different targets and priority areas so as to steer the economic development of the country. Modernising and transforming the agricultural sector were the main targets and key priority areas in all the plans. The first two plans paved the way[6] for realising FDI in large-scale commercial farming, which was extensively practised during the third plan. During this plan, domestic industries such as food processing and textile and sugar production were established and operationalised by foreign (such as by the British, Dutch and Americans) and domestic investors to process the agricultural raw materials as the starting point for the agricultural transformation (Negarit Gazette, 1949, 1954, 1966; IEG, 1962; MoI, 1973). The regime encouraged FDI in agriculture through various incentives such as tax relief, long-term land lease with a low rental fee, provision of a loan under favourable conditions and remittance of funds (IEG, 1962).

5.3 FDI during the military regime: policies and practices

The military regime, called Dergue (meaning "a committee of soldiers"), declared socialism as its main doctrine. Soon after taking power in 1974, the military government nationalised all private-owned businesses including commercial farms, which were mainly owned by foreigners. The government also implemented a new rural and urban land reform programme (Negarit Gazette, No. 22, 1975; Negarit Gazette, No. 31, 1975; Negarit Gazette, No. 47, 1975; Henze, 2000). Since 1975, all large-scale agricultural investments were owned by the government. These investments were administered by various agricultural development corporations which were governed by Public Enterprises Proclamation and Regulation Nos. 20/1975 and 5/1975, respectively (Negarit Gazette, No. 21, 1976). In the same year, the military government directed that certain specific activities such as mining, processing food products and large-scale construction works were to be undertaken jointly by the government and foreign investors. However, the share of the foreign investor was less than 49% and large-scale agricultural activities were solely for state ownership (Negarit Gazette, No. 21, 1976).

A number of large state farms were established during this regime. The government also tried to arrange agriculture through the organisation of individual farm units in peasant associations (PAs). The PAs roles were allocating and reallocating land for households, collecting taxes and determining production quotas, and organising voluntary labour for public works. The PAs, in turn, established service cooperatives whose functions were to supply market and extend agricultural services. There were also producers' cooperatives (PCs), which were composed of individual households that commonly managed their consolidated farms. However, the regime efforts were directed towards the "socialisation" of agriculture and were not fully realised due to the strong resistance from peasants against joining the PCs. Hence, the structure of production remained mainly private. After 15 years of the regime's rule, the share of private holdings in the total cultivated land was about 94%, while the rest was divided between PCs (2.5%) and state farms (3.5%; FAO, 1993b).

The regime was confronted with crises throughout its term in power. In the beginning, there were groups who attempted to overthrow the military regime which caused mass bloodshed (the Ethiopian Red Terror).[7] The regime also fought two parallel civil wars with the Eritrean People's Liberation Force (EPLF)[8] and the Tigray People's Liberation Front (TPLF)[9] and a border war with Somalia (Turner, 1993; Ethiopian Treasures, 2015). The dramatic global political shifts in the late 1980s, particularly the end of the Cold War,[10] threatened to isolate the military regime from its allies such as the Soviet Union (Turner, 1993). This turning point forced the government to acknowledge the failure of the command economy and to reform its economic policy. In 1990, the government proposed to implement a mixed economy model, which allowed the participation of foreign investments in all parts of the economy, including agriculture, without a capital investment limit (see Special Decree No. 17/1990, and Regulation No. 10/1990). However, the history of confiscating private properties, including private commercial farms, as well as the political instability of the country, discouraged the inflow of FDI (Henze, 2000; Astatike and Assefa, 2005).

5.4 FDI during the EPRDF regime: policies and practices

The EPRDF regime, which came into power in 1991 and like its predecessors, advocates for agricultural development as the economic pillar of Ethiopia. In the early 1990s, the regime developed the ADLI strategy as its macroeconomic policy framework to achieve its long-term economic and social development goals. This strategy had, for about 20 years, been a master plan providing for rural infrastructure and social development programmes in order to realise agricultural development. It laid the foundation for all Ethiopian policies and strategies that were designed afterwards to facilitate agricultural and rural transformation (MoFED, 2003). The strategy focused on strengthening the capacity of smallholder farmers to increase production and productivity while encouraging the private sector to engage in large-scale agricultural investment to contribute to the production of sufficient food for domestic consumption and cash crops for export (MoFED, 2010).

The EPRDF government also undertook economic policy reform, which allowed the transformation from a command economy system, in which the economy had been regulated and restricted by the government to a market-oriented economy, in which the economy is operated by voluntary exchange in a free market rather than controlled by the government. This economic liberalisation has been encouraging greater private-sector involvement, including private investments, in large-scale agriculture (MoFED, 2003). It strongly believes that FDI in large-scale agriculture will: support the expansion of production in order to secure food for the country, provide employment to the unemployed workforce, transfer technology to smallholder farmers, develop infrastructure, boost export of agricultural products and increase foreign earning (MoFED, 2003). In addition, many donors, particularly the World Bank, have been urging the Ethiopian government to favour agricultural commercialisation (World Bank, 2010). As a result, there has been a significant increase of FDI inflows to Ethiopia during the EPRDF government and the ongoing effect of the economic reforms.

In view of promoting FDI, therefore, in 1994, the government established the Ethiopian Privatisation Agency to facilitate the transferring of state-owned enterprises to domestic and foreign investors (Astatike and Assefa, 2005). Accordingly, transfers of state-owned enterprises to investors have been taking place through tendering (Leykun, 2013). In addition to the previously noted privatisation programmes (PPESA, 2014), the government established various institutions to support the implementation of the Investment Policy that strongly advocates for FDI. Those institutions include the Ethiopian Investment Agency (ETIA; Proclamation No. 769/2012), which was later reconstituted as the Ethiopian Investment Commission (EIC; Proc. No. 313/2014) and the Ethiopian Agricultural Investment Land Administration Agency (EAILAA; Negarit Gazette, 2013). Investors, mainly foreigners, that aspire to engage in export crops production have been encouraged through tax incentives, as well as priority access to land and water sources for irrigation (ETIA, 2013; Proc. No. 313/2014).

The recent influx of foreign investors in large-scale agriculture from India, Saudi Arabia and Turkey (EAILAA, 2014) into Ethiopia is stimulated not only by the change in Ethiopia's economic policy and political stability (ETIA, 2013) but also by the global demand for agricultural products since the global food and financial crisis of 2007 and 2008 (Görgon et al., 2009).

The government's generosity in allocating a huge tract of fertile lands has also been a big attraction for foreign investors. In this regard, Cotula et al. (2009) reveal that, since 2004, Ethiopia is the first among the African countries that allocated prime farmlands to foreign investors. The allocation in Ethiopia accounted for 15% of the total land area under FDI in agriculture in SSA, followed by Mozambique whose allocation amounted to 11% of the total land area allocated to foreign investors (AMCOW, 2014). In Ethiopia, FDI in agriculture, manufacturing and services increased by 16% from 1992 to 2012 (ETIA, 2013).

In addition to the policy and institutional incentives, the lowness of land-lease prices is another pull factor for foreign investors that engage in large-scale agriculture. For instance, Cotula (2012) argues that in Ethiopia, an acre of land can be leased for less than US$1 per year while in Asia it costs more than US$100. Furthermore, the Ethiopian government has not put in place mechanisms to ensure that these investments play a positive role in improving food security, transferring technology and improving the living standards of local people, especially those of smallholder farmers; neither did it set limits on water use, enforce EIAs and ensure the payment of compensation to displaced people (Oakland Institute, 2011). All the foregoing is to attract foreign investors to embark on large-scale agriculture.

From the host country's context, the Oakland Institute concluded that these investments are not being carried out in a way that safeguards the social, environmental and food security needs of the local populations. Huge discrepancies were also noted between publicly stated positions, laws, policies and procedures, and what is actually happening on the ground (Oakland Institute, 2011). This concern is echoed by Rahmato's (2011) study, as well.

5.5 Similarities and differences among the three regimes' agricultural investment policies: reflections on their implications

Although the three regimes have different ideologies and approaches, their economic policies have similarities when it comes to advancing the development of the agricultural sector. The majority of Ethiopians (about 85%) still live in the rural areas and are engaged in small-scale farming. Subsistence farming is still widely practised in Ethiopia.

The contribution of the agricultural sector to the GDP was higher in the imperial and military regimes compared to the current EPRDF government (Gish et al., 2007). The investment policies of the imperial regime encouraged FDI in large-scale agriculture. This has been continued by the current EPRDF government. The investment policy of the former military government, however, did not allow FDI in agriculture until the change of the economic system at the end of its tenure (see Table 5.1)

The imperial government discouraged the export of agricultural raw materials through imposing export tax while the current government doesn't impose a tax on export of agricultural products. The reason for the imperial government imposing an export tax on agricultural raw materials was to encourage the establishment of domestic industry and to export processed goods that were exempted from export tax. During the imperial regime, an out-growers scheme was practised to encourage linkages of FDI with domestic farmers and increase FDI spillover effects. This is not practised by the current government (see Table 5.1).

The percentage of the population engaged in agriculture is similar in all regimes (Photius, 2015). The size of the population tripled in the EPRDF regime (96 million) compared to in imperial times (28 million). It has doubled in the EPRDF regime compared to the military regime (48 million; Worldometers, 2015). Because the percentage of people engaged in agriculture is static, the number of people that are engaged in agriculture is highest in the EPRDF regime. This, in turn, means that the size of the agricultural land area per individual farmer is significantly reduced today compared to historically under the previous two regimes (see Table 5.1).

5.6 Summary

This chapter has documented that the history of FDI in agriculture dates back to 1930, when Emperor Haile Selassie I came to power. During the military regime, from 1974 to 1991, FDI in large-scale agriculture was discouraged as the administration focused on the promotion of state-owned large farms. The EPRDF government, which succeeded the military regime in 1991, encourages FDI in agriculture, and that is evident from its agricultural and rural development policies and strategies.

All the three regimes acknowledged the importance of agriculture in the Ethiopian economy and advocated for the development of the sector as the economic

Table 5.1 Similarities and Differences Among Investment Policies of the Imperial, Military and EPRDF Regimes

	Imperial Regime 1930–74	Military Regime 1974–91	EPRDF Regime 1991 to date
Political System **Economic System**	Feudal/Capitalism Market Economy	Socialism/Communism Command Economy (1974–90)/Mixed Economy (1990–91)[1]	Ethnic Federalism Market Economy
Total population **Population density** **Population engaged in agriculture**	28,414,999 in July 1970 26 per sq km in 1970 86% in 1973	48,042,755 in July 1990 44 per sq km in 1990 80% in 1991	96,506,031 in July 2014 87 per sq km in 2014 85% in 2014
Agriculture contribution to GDP **Agriculture contribution to Export**	60% in 1973 90% in 1973	57% in 1991 80% in 1991	47.7% in 2014 90% in 2011
Investment Policy	Allowed FDI in agriculture	Did not allow FDI in agriculture until 1990	Allows FDI in agriculture
Incentives to attract FDI	– Five years income tax relief on investment above Eth Dollar 200,000 – Exemption from import tax – 2% export tax on agricultural raw materials while manufactured-finished goods are exempted from export tax – Remittance of funds – Provision of 30% domestic credits under favourable conditions – Long-term tenancy of the land for symbolic rental fee	– Three years income tax relief on investment over Eth Birr 300,000 but not exceeding 750,000 – Four years income tax relief on investment over Eth 750,000 but not exceeding 2,000,000 – Six years income tax relief on investment over Eth 2,000,000 – Exemption from import tax – Remittance of funds – No provision of domestic credits – Limited time land lease	– 30% income tax relief for maximum 3 to 6 years depending on the distance from Addis Ababa – Exemption from import tax – Exemption from export tax – Remittance of funds – Provision of 70% domestic credits under favourable conditions – Long-term land lease for cheap rental fee
Capital requirement	There is no stated minimum capital requirement	Total investment capital	Minimum capital USD 200,000 for a single investment project
Major products	– Cotton – Sugarcane – Tobacco	Not specified	– Pongami for biofuel – Cotton – Rice
Out-growers scheme	Practised	Not practised	Not yet practised

[1]The economic policy change to a mixed economy went into effect on May 1990 by the Council of Special Decree No. 17/1990 and Council of Ministers Regulation No. 10/1990.

pillar of Ethiopia. However, the strategy they applied to develop the sector varied from regime to regime, as dictated by their macroeconomic policies and political economy.

It's worth noting that the Ethiopian population has increased exponentially during the last 25 years. This increase implies that the size of land allocated for the local individual smallholder farmer is less than the previous regime. If the current government doesn't put in place measures to control the population growth, the size of land for individual farmer will continue to shrink further and risks the population food sufficiency. Besides, the government should be mindful of the growing population and needs to reassess its encouragement for export-oriented FDI in large-scale commercial farming which doesn't directly respond to the growing Ethiopian population food needs. Furthermore, the government needs to consider its response to the global demand on climate change when granting long-term leases for huge tracts of forestlands to FDI in agriculture.

Notes

1 Before 1991, Ethiopia had the Red Sea ports. The independence of Eritrea in 1991 made Ethiopia a landlocked country.
2 The Great Depression was a severe worldwide economic depression in the 1930s.
3 For example dams, roads, buildings and communications.
4 For example formal education, training of technical personnel and training of social workers to serve villages and districts.
5 First plan (1957–62), Second plan (1963–67), and Third plan (1968–73).
6 During these periods, the government formulated a series of policies such as land concession, ownership, investment and tax incentives to encourage FDI in large-scale agriculture.
7 The Ethiopian Red Terror took place in 1977–78 after the military government "Dergue" took power, and it was a violent political campaign where students involved.
8 Eritrea gained independence in 1991 after the overthrown of the military government "Dergue".
9 The TPLF, operating as the chief member of a coalition called the EPRDF, has been leading Ethiopia since the overthrow of the military government "Dergue" in 1991.
10 The end of the Cold War resulted in the dissolution of the Union of Soviet Socialist Republics (USSR) and democratic reform in Eastern Europe.

6 Ethiopian policies, strategies and institutions that promote FDI in large-scale agriculture

6.1 Introduction

As mentioned in Sections 3.9.3 and 4.4, the current Ethiopian government has set in place a number of policies and institutions that are meant to promote and facilitate the operation of inward FDI in large-scale agriculture. The main of those is the investment policy, the essences of which have been streamlined in the different sectoral policies. This chapter discusses the contents of the current investment policy in relation to FDI in large-scale agriculture, as well as its implementation. In addition, it discusses the institutions that are mandated to promote and to facilitate the operation of inward FDI in large-scale agriculture.

The contents of the Ethiopian investment policy and agricultural land-lease agreement terms and conditions were assessed by using as reference points the global and regional frameworks and guidelines in national investment policies, strategies, laws, rules and programmes for effective and sustainable agricultural sector development (see Sections 3.9.1 and 3.9.2). In addition, empirical findings of works on agricultural transformation processes (see Section 3.2) are used to further assess the Ethiopian investment policy with regard to pro-poor and environmentally sustainable agricultural transformation. Empirical findings about the roles of host country FDI policies and best practices are used to analyze the support in practice of the Ethiopian investment policy for pro-poor and environmentally sustainable FDI in large-scale agriculture (see Sections 3.7 and 3.8). The key investment promotion institutions that facilitate inward FDI in agriculture are assessed using the institutional framework for adequate investment promotion (see Sections 2.4.1 and 2.4.2).

6.2 Policies and strategies that support FDI in large-scale agriculture in Ethiopia

Since the adoption of the ADLI strategy, Ethiopia formulated and adopted a number of economic and social development policies and strategies to facilitate agricultural transformation. The Rural Development Policy and Strategy (RDPS) is the most aligned to ADLI and the basis for other policies and policy-based proclamations that promote FDI in large-scale agriculture. These include the Rural

Land Administration and Land Use Proclamation, Investment Proclamation, the Growth and Transformation Plan (GTP), Education Policy, Health Policy, Infrastructure Policy, Labour Policy, Environmental Policy and National Social Protection Policy. This section discusses the contents of the current policies with respect to their support for pro-poor and environmentally sustainable FDI in agriculture in Ethiopia.

6.2.1 *Rural development policy and strategies*

Rural Development Policy and Strategies (2003) underscores the importance of foreign investments in the agricultural sector to enhance the agricultural development efforts. These investments are encouraged in the sparsely populated lowland areas that have a high potential for large-scale agriculture. The policy supports the leasing of land to facilitate foreign investments in these areas. This is also supported by the Rural Land Administration and Land Use Proclamation No. 456/2005, Article 5 – Acquisition and Use of Rural Land, Sub-Articles 4 (a) and (b).

The policy is sound in content and captures aspects that have significance in leading to rural and agricultural transformation. It encourages sustainable and pro-poor FDI in large-scale agriculture, specifically in lowland areas which require a significant amount of development. The policy recognises the insufficiency of incentives to attract FDI and stresses the important aspects that facilitate FDI's operation and make FDI conducive to Ethiopia's development. These aspects include development of infrastructure, the provision of health services (especially the control of malaria), the upgrading of the skills of agricultural labour, the promotion of labour-intensive technology to adequately use the abundant labour, the sustainable use of natural resources and the creation of direct linkages between agricultural investors and local smallholder farmers through an "out-grower scheme". The policy further favours the establishment of an efficient agricultural marketing system to facilitate that Ethiopia's agricultural products penetrate external markets and improve its market share while offering timely and accurate information on the price and volume, as well as low transaction costs to attract further FDI. The importance of the aspects that were captured by the Rural Development Policy were confirmed by various studies (see Sections 3.6 and 3.9.3).

The Rural Development Policy is time-cognisant and planned the agricultural transformation differently compared to countries that transformed their agriculture more than a century ago. For instance, it planned the agricultural transformation to be in a parallel rather than in a stepped or phased approach[1] like in North America, Japan and Western Europe.[2] The policy supports agricultural research and extension programmes and strategic input supply to increase productivity and transform the subsistence environment into one of diversified agriculture, especially in the densely populated highland areas with many subsistence farmers. At the same time, it encourages FDI in large-scale commercial farming in sparsely populated lowland areas with the view to expedite agricultural transformation (see Section 3.2). This policy's approach is tailored to Ethiopia's needs to ensure food security for the country's growing population and to increase foreign earnings while responding to the global demand for agricultural products such as food and biofuel crops.

6.2.2 *Rural land administration proclamation*

The Rural Land Administration Proclamation No. 456/2005 explicitly supports foreign direct investment in large-scale agriculture. Article 5, Sub-Article 4 (a) and (b) state that

> *[p]rivate investors that engage in agricultural development activities shall have the right to use rural land in accordance with the investment policies and laws at federal and regional levels,* Sub-Article 4(a); *and Governmental and non-governmental organizations and social and economic institutions shall have the right to use rural land in line with their development objectives,* Sub-Article 4(b).

Articles 7(3), 8 and 11(3 and 4) of the Rural Land Administration and Land Use Proclamation re-emphasises the policy's support for agricultural investment.

The proclamation demonstrates support for sustainable FDI in large-scale agriculture. It attempts to create an enabling environment for agricultural development through the facilitation of agricultural land leases. Further, it recognises the negative impact of large-scale farming on the natural environment and gives provision in Article 13 to protect the environment from large-scale agricultural activities. It delineates responsibilities to federal and regional levels of government, thus conforming to Articles 50 and 92 of the Constitution, respectively. It also stresses the establishment and strengthening of existing institutions of land administration and using management to ensure compliance at the local level. The attention to the environmental impacts of agricultural activities is also in line with the Environmental Impact Assessment Proclamation No. 299/2002 and the AUC–AfDB–UNECA Joint Land Policy Initiative (2007) background document on land policy in Africa. Delineating responsibilities as well as strengthening institutional capacities can enhance the sustainability, effectiveness and efficiency of services, thus facilitating adequate operation of FDI. In addition, quality services such as formulating and enforcing contracts as well as engagement of FDI-promoting local institutions in educating foreign investors on country's various potential locations for FDI and their specific economic advantages can positively impact economic activities through the low transaction and production costs (see Section 2.4).

Although this book recognises the proclamation's many positive aspects, it has a number of areas that need improvement. There is a need to avoid misinterpretation and land conflicts. The provision in Article 5(4) "the right to use rural land in line with investors' development objectives" may undermine the prioritisation of Ethiopia's development objectives against foreign investors' as both clearly have different development objectives. The provision in Article 7 "eviction of smallholder farmers' land for public use" contradicts the provisions in Articles 8(1) and 11(3 and 5):

> *Voluntary agreements of smallholder farmers to transfer their lands use right to an investor for a limited time, facilitate land consolidation, settlement and villagisation programme for agricultural development.*

In fact, encouraging the voluntary agreement of people to facilitate the settlement and villagisation programme was stressed in the Rural Development Policy which recognises that moving people by force is not productive and can create social turmoil.

The inconsistency of the various articles of the proclamation, especially the part pertaining to the land-tenure insecurity of smallholder farmers and rural dwellers, could be a major problem for facilitating pro-poor agricultural investment in Ethiopia. This inconsistency needs to be removed so as to balance the rights and interests of all land users to enable them to realise full social, environmental and economic benefits from land, as well as to contribute to Ethiopia's agricultural development.

This book recognises that the term *public use* which was used in Article 7, dealing with the eviction of smallholder farmers in order to use their land for public use, was given neither an operational definition in the proclamation nor a reference to other public documents. This lack of clarity may lead to different interpretations by implementers, possibly leading to an inefficient and ineffective realisation of the objective of ADLI. Such inconsistency hampers the consistent and effective execution of policies, thereby limiting the positive effects of FDI (i.e. economic growth, skill upgrading and capital; see also Section 2.4.1).

6.2.3 Investment proclamation

The Investment Proclamation No. 769/2012 clearly articulates its support for FDI in Article 5 where it states the role of foreign investment in Ethiopia's economic development. To encourage FDI, the Proclamation further emphasises the investment incentives, guarantees and protection, and remittance of funds in its Articles 23, 24, 25 and 26. The study recognises that the Proclamation attempts to attract inward FDI, but there are areas that require major improvements so as to promote Ethiopia's long-term development agenda.

Although incentives are a vital element to attract inward FDI, this study notes that the generous investment incentives, especially for export-oriented agricultural investments, are granted up front without sufficient conditions in favour of Ethiopia and its citizens. The incentives include long-term loans with very low interest rates, the ability to lease large tracts of land for half a century with very low lease prices and four- to five-year grace periods, tax exemptions[3] and residence permits. The conditions for incentives could enable Ethiopia to ascertain some of the envisaged investment benefits such as skills upgrading through training as well as creating linkages between foreign investors and local smallholder farmers. In addition, if incentives are tied to the performance of the investment projects, Ethiopia could be able to neutralise the loss in the event that projects do not perform as predicted (see Section 2.4.7.).

In this study, it is observed that the Proclamation facilitates the application for an investment permit by a foreign investor using a form designed for such purpose. However, the information requested in the stated application form is general and does not have local content requirements and does not seek information that could allow distinguishing between speculative and long-term investors. It also does not have aspects of investors' previous experience in the requested investment project as well as investors' track records in terms of environmental and social performance of their previous investments. Once a foreign investor allocates the minimum capital require-ment (US$200,000) for an investment project, the said entity is granted the invest-ment permit and the incentives immediately. This investment promotion to attract inward FDI may have negative consequences for Ethiopia, such as compromising the country's security as any person in the pretext of investment can enter into the coun-try and promote anti-peace activities such as terrorist attacks, which is the case in the Horn of Africa (e.g. by Al-Shabaab). An investor's track records and past experience could be an indicator to ensure the project's social, environmental and economic per-formance provided that all other things remain the same (see Section 2.4.8).

This study also identifies that Article 38 in the proclamation, which specifies that it is the duty of the investor to protect the environment, is in breach of the constitutional provision of Article 92 (4) that states that "government and citizens shall have the duty to protect the environment". This inconsistency is bound to create a challenge to implementers of this proclamation and may prove ineffective in the long run.

6.2.4 Education and training policy

The Education and Training Policy was designed to promote the ADLI strategy. The policy-specific objectives include the promotion of relevant and appropriate education and training through formal and informal programmes, the provision of training in various skills and at different levels so as to satisfy the country's need for skilled human power, as well as the provision of education that promotes the culture of respect for work, positive work habits and high regard for workmanship.

The overall policy approach is adequate to equip the workforce with the required skills to facilitate FDI operation in Ethiopia. The policy attempts to address the education and training needs of Ethiopia. It recognises the huge workforce of Ethiopia and tries to design education and training that corresponds with Ethio-pia's current need to achieve the development objective. It also realises the need for financial resources for the provision of the various levels of education, training and research and has put in a strategy to fund these programmes.

The most apparent education and training areas that the policy focuses on are agriculture, health, infrastructure and entrepreneurial skills. These fields of educa-tion and skills are critical to attracting FDI, to facilitate its operation, to absorb the labour force and, for domestic firms, to capture the positive effects of FDI. This will ensure long-lasting benefits for Ethiopia. In addition, aligning education, training and research to the specific needs of investment areas is one of the success criteria for attracting FDI. A large number of scholars underline the importance of education, training, research and a skilled workforce in encouraging inward FDI.

They also highlight the availability of a skilled labour force and labour productivity as determining factors for inward FDI decision. The education policy of equipping students in more than two languages, including English, directly supports inward FDI operations in Ethiopia (see Section 2.4.3).

6.2.5 Health policy and strategies

The Health Policy (1993) reiterates the overall development objective of the country (i.e. agricultural transformation). The policy acknowledges the importance of health for economic growth and emphasises health promotion that is in many ways economical rather than curative. It emphasises the significant role of a healthy population in advancing social and economic development. A healthy population and a productive workforce are the determinant factors for FDI inflows, especially labour-efficiency-seeking FDI. The policy acknowledges that health is a fundamental element for Ethiopia's development. Improved health enhances students' learning capacity which promotes the education policy implementation. This, in turn, promotes a skilled workforce that advances economic development. This positive effect of the host country's population health in attracting FDI inflows is noted by many scholars (see Section 2.4.6).

In addition, the health policy highlights the need to prevent and control pandemic and endemic communicable diseases such as HIV/AIDS, tuberculosis and malaria. It has put strategies such as the Health Extension Programme[4] in place to curb the problems. This strategy is in line with the investment policy, which encourages large-scale agricultural investments in lowland areas that are malaria-prone and requires extensive health services to prevent and control such diseases and ensure labour productivity. Strengthening the health system is also an important factor to encourage FDI as it ensures the control and managing of disease outbreaks which could deter inward FDI flow as experienced in the recent deadly Ebola disease in West Africa. The correlation of population health with economic performance, as well as between disease outbreaks and FDI flows, has been documented by many scholars (see Section 2.4.6).

6.2.6 Infrastructure development programme

The Macroeconomic Policy Framework in Ethiopia also includes infrastructure development, which is key to the development of various sectors to advance the social and economic development of the country. The development of infrastructure, such as transportation, communications and electric power facilities, very important to ensure accelerated economic growth. The Macroeconomic Policy Framework stresses the infrastructure sector's important role in contributing to the development of the agricultural and industrial sectors.

As a result, the government has set the infrastructure development programme. The programme is further necessitated by the investment policy which spells out the needed infrastructure for lowland areas where large-scale agricultural investments are encouraged. This programme directly supports FDI in large-scale agriculture. The infrastructure development programme in lowland areas and the need for large amounts of capital for undertaking the various infrastructure development projects are acknowledged in the Rural Development Policy and the GTP, which have also put in place a strategy to obtain the required resources.

The World Bank study on Ethiopia's infrastructure (Foster and Morella, 2011), as well as the AfDB group's Country Strategy (AfDB, 2011), confirms the need for intensification of infrastructure development in Ethiopia. It has become one of the Ethiopian government's priority areas in order to sustain Ethiopia's high economic growth and to increase competitiveness. The direct engagement of the Ethiopian government in infrastructure development also contributes to attracting inward FDI. This has been validated by many scholars (see Section 2.4.4).

6.2.7 Labour proclamation

Ethiopia has been a member of the International Labour Organization (ILO) since 1923 and has ratified major conventions of the ILO, which demand that Ethiopia commit itself to upholding the core labour standards (Redea, 2009; OSAHD, Pers., Fed., 2014). These include the prohibition against child labour, prohibition of forced labour, the right to organised and collective bargaining, freedom from discrimination in employment and remuneration, as well as occupational safety and health, which have been re-emphasised in the National Employment Policy and Strategy, designed to advance the implementation of the Labour Proclamation.

The Labour Proclamation No. 377/2003 and subsequent revised proclamations (Nos. 466/2005 and 494/2006) support FDI through the established labour standards that are based on international labour standards. Furthermore, Ethiopia is promoting labour-intensive technology with the view of creating employment for the abundant labour. These labour standards protect the agricultural workers' fundamental rights such as negotiating of an employment contract, working hours, overtime pay, leave and wages. The occupational health, safety and working environment standards in agriculture also protect agricultural workers' rights. They are meant to attract socially responsible inward FDI (see Sections 2.4.3 and 2.4.5).

6.2.8 Environmental policy

The Ethiopian Environmental Policy addresses a wide range of environment-related issues,[5] including sectoral and cross-sectoral environmental concerns, in a comprehensive manner. The policy's overall objective is to ensure the sustainable use of natural, human-made and cultural resources as well as to promote sustainable social and economic development. The policy directs each economic and social sector to develop and implement their sector-specific environmental policies and associated directives and guidelines, as well as to monitor, evaluate and review the regulatory frameworks. The policy advocates for community participation in all phases of environmental and resource development and management, the protection of cultural and natural heritage and LUP, EIAs and strategic environmental assessments (SEAs).

The environmental policy of Ethiopia is in agreement with the various international environment-related conventions that Ethiopia is a signatory to. The policy fully promotes sustainable FDI in agriculture through its provisions. It has paved the way for many environment-related proclamations, regulations and strategies, such as the Environmental Impact Assessment Proclamation, Environmental Pollution Control Proclamation, Solid Waste Management Proclamation, Industrial Pollution Regulation, Climate Resilient Green Economy Strategy and the upgrading of the Environmental Protection Authority to ministry level. These policy instruments are proactive tools to harmonise policies and to integrate environmental, economic, cultural and social considerations into decision-making processes in a manner that promotes sustainable development.

In addition, the policy is considerate in its balance of environmental, social and economic concerns through its provisions of citizens' fundamental rights.[6] These are enshrined in Article 43 of the Constitution (The Right to Development),[7] Article 44 (Environmental Rights),[8] and Article 92 (Environmental Objectives).[9] It underscores the importance of strategic LUP and EIA. These involve a wide range of disciplines and engagement with communities that are likely to be affected by the decision. It aims to efficiently and objectively regulate land use and avoid land-use conflicts so as to advance sustainable development. The policy is sensitive to the current Ethiopian development challenges of food security, mitigating and adapting to climate change, protecting biodiversity whilst promoting economic growth and preventing and settling land conflicts.

A large body of literature also confirms the Ethiopian Environmental Policy to be transparent and in accordance with the sustainable development principles and international environmental standards that are designed to promote environmental sustainability while ensuring economic and social development (Krueger et al., 2012; Tesfaye, 2008; Ruffeis et al., 2010). Several studies confirm that environmental standards encourage environmentally responsible inward FDI (see Section 2.4.5).

6.2.9 Social protection policy

Ethiopia has signed a number of international and continental agreements related to social development, which encompass social protection. These agreements include the Universal Declaration of Human Rights (UDHR), the International Covenant on Economic, Social and Cultural Rights and the African Union Social Policy Framework for Africa. Article 9(4) of the Ethiopian Constitution authorised all international agreements ratified by Ethiopia to be an integral part of the national law. The Constitution further gives a specific provision for social protection in its Article 90. The National Social Protection Policy, which is based on the ADLI principles and focuses mainly on reducing agricultural vulnerabilities, supports FDI in agriculture through its provision for social protection that improves the effectiveness and efficiency of investments. This, in turn, accelerates the attainment of the development goals of Ethiopia, especially for the most vulnerable members of society who are mainly found in the lowland rural areas where FDI in large-scale agriculture is encouraged. Many scholars have documented the wide range of long-lasting benefits from effective social protection such as improved security, sustained peace and greater social stability, which significantly contribute to attracting inward FDI (see Section 2.4.2).

6.2.10 Growth and transformation plans I and II

The essences of the foregoing policies related to FDI in large-scale agriculture have been reflected in different short and mid-term development plans. Notable references of those policy provisions are made in the Growth and Transformation Plan I (GTP I) five-year (2011–15) and GTP II (2016–2020; NPC, 2016). These documents are medium-term strategic frameworks that echoed the Rural Development Policy and Strategies and re-emphasised the importance of foreign investment in large-scale agriculture to advance agricultural development in Ethiopia. The plans urged that particularly export-oriented large-scale farming such as cotton, date palms, tea and rubber tree plantations should be actively supported.

It is natural for the GTP I and II to encourage export-oriented agricultural investments in line with Ethiopia's Investment Policy. The Plans do not relate export-orientation with the spillover effects of FDI. Unintended effects could relate to the fact that the agricultural sector is still in its infancy and the smallholder farmers apply primitive tools. It is likely that they are not adequately capacitated to take up the positive externalities of FDI in highly mechanised large-scale agricultural ventures (see Section 2.4.1).

The GTP I and II stress the expansion of quality education and health services, which are vital elements to encourage inward FDI. The GTP I, for instance, highlights the available land (about three million hectares within the five-year period) for large-scale commercial farming, which is a determinant factor for FDI in agriculture. The GTPs promote labour-intensive technology as Ethiopia has abundant labour. These plans enable to reflect on the policy objectives of each sector, including agriculture sector policies, and their harmonisation. It is a good tool to track progress and take corrective action in a timely manner.

Although the GTPs I and II advocate for labour-intensive technology, the absorption of labour is dependent on the investment type, that is capital-intensive or labour-intensive. It is well-known that the large-scale agricultural projects in Ethiopia are capital-intensive, and thus, their demand for labour is limited (see Sections 2.4.3 and 3.5).

6.3 Institutions that facilitate FDI in large-scale agriculture in Ethiopia

Institutional and regulatory frameworks are vital elements to encourage inward FDI. Hence, Ethiopia established three FDI promotion institutions that are at the forefront and play a pivotal role in facilitating the implementation of the investment policy in large-scale agriculture. The Ethiopian Investment Commission (EIC)[10] was established to implement a transparent and efficient investment administration system with the view to encourage and expand foreign investments. The

EAILAA[11] was established to administer large-scale agricultural investments, and the Development Bank of Ethiopia (DBE)[12] is mandated to promote the national development agenda through the provision of development finance and technical support to viable projects that are in government's priority areas, such as agriculture. Figure 6.1 describes the different functions and sequences carried out by these three institutions to facilitate FDI in large-scale agriculture.

These institutions promote FDI along with generous incentives, which, compounded with the current high global demand for agricultural products, encourage

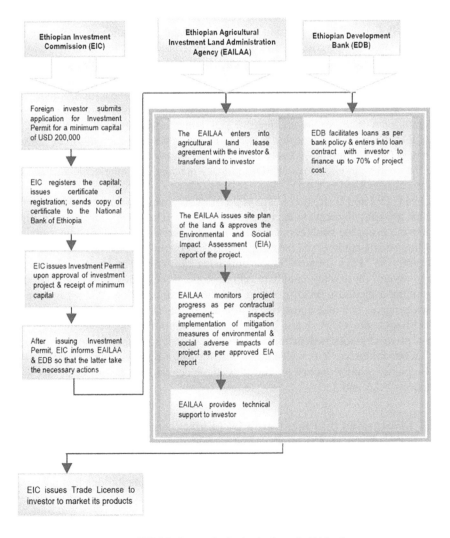

Figure 6.1 Process Tree of FDI in Large-Scale Agriculture in Ethiopia

the flow of FDI in agriculture to Ethiopia. The facilitation of FDI operations once established in Ethiopia requires the availability of the technical and financial capacity of these institutions. Furthermore, the competence of these institutions has a significant impact on the quantity and quality of attracted FDI in agriculture into Ethiopia. The DBE has almost a century of experience in financing development projects and programmes and it may have the required capacity in facilitating the financing of the agricultural projects in the form of long-term loans. The EIC and EILAA are in their infancy and require strengthening their human and financial capacity to adequately carry out their mandates (EPD, Pers., Fed., 2014; EIAT, Pers., Fed., 2014; AEZ, Pers., Fed., 2014; ISEMED, Pers., Fed., 2014; LEAD, Pers., Fed., 2014; LAD, Pers., Fed., 2014; IPST, Pers., Fed, 2014; AIPFAT, Pers., Fed., 2014).[13]

The social and economic sector institutions that are also crucial for the facilitation and scrutiny of sustainable and pro-poor agricultural investments include health, education, labour, environment, infrastructure and policing. The need for human and financial capacity of these institutions is evident from the challenges faced in the implementation of the various policies that are designed to facilitate FDI in large-scale agriculture.

6.4 Agricultural land lease agreements: terms, conditions, content and intent

The format of the current Ethiopian agricultural land-lease agreement requires information about identity, signature and contact information of both parties (Lessor and Lessee), purpose of the agreement, description of the property (farmland), lease term with start and end dates (duration of lease period), method and amount of land rent per annum and permitted and prohibited uses of the leased land. It also requires the lessee's rights and obligations, the lessor's rights and obligations, the conditions to transfer land leaseholder's right to a third party, the contract's termination and renewals conditions, the contract's termination grounds and procedures, disputes settlement, communication modalities, the validity of the contract and its registration, the contract's governing law and governing conditions of force majeure.

This land-lease agreement format is very loose in addressing the crucial and obvious social and environmental problems related to large-scale agriculture. It excludes essential clauses, such as farm insurance to cover pollution and environmental liability, conservation plans, conditions of the farmland on return, arrangements for compensation, maintenance and repair of the farmland, security deposit, monitoring and reporting format and frequency, non-point source pollution, the number and type of jobs to be created for the locals and engagement with the local smallholder farmers to improve their farming methods.

The agricultural land-lease agreements are one of the instruments to implement policies, policy-based proclamations, directives and guidelines that are designed to promote agricultural and rural development in Ethiopia. The lease agreement should, therefore, mirror these policies to facilitate their adequate implementation.

It should make emphasis on the social and environmental consequences of large-scale commercial agriculture and make a clear provision of responsibilities and obligations of land leaseholders (i.e. investors), as well as landowners (Ethiopian government), in order to bring social, economic and ecological benefits, such as soil conservation, water quality, air quality, flood damage mitigation, maintaining and improving biodiversity and wildlife habitat and mitigating against global warming. It is imperative to carefully assess the terms and conditions of agricultural land lease contracts vis-à-vis economic, social and environmental benefits for Ethiopia. This argument is supported by many studies that stress agricultural land-lease agreements are critical aspects of agricultural production and marketing. It defines the landowners and the land leaseholders' responsibilities and obligations, which are legally binding. These responsibilities and obligations of both parties should encompass the elements for sustainable and pro-poor investments in agricultural lands so as to ensure social stability, environmental sustainability, peace and security (see Sections 3.7, 3.8 and 3.9).

6.5 Practical challenges in implementing policies that support FDI in agriculture in Ethiopia

This section presents the fundamental problems that the institutions tasked with investment promotion face in their efforts to effectively carry out their mandates. It also reports on the major challenges to implementing the policies as evidenced by the poor performance of large-scale agricultural investment projects (see Section 7.3.2).

The principal implementing agencies of the investment policy lack financial and human resources and technical capacity (PMELD, Pers., Fed., 2014; IPST, Pers., Fed., 2014; AIPFAT, Pers., Fed., 2014; EPD, Pers., Fed., 2014; LAD, Pers., Fed., 2014; EPU, Pers., Reg., 2014; LUAU, Pers., Reg., 2014; see Appendix 1 for these references codes). The lack of technical and financial capacity of the investment promotion agencies at all levels of government (federal, regional, district and kebele)[14] hampers the ability to facilitate the operation of the agricultural investment projects. This includes the institutions capacity to carry out adequate LUP and financial valuation of land (LAD, Pers., Fed., 2014; EIAT, Pers., Fed., 2014). The tasks require expertise and skills within the institutions and the local knowledge of the community. Adequate lease agreements (see Sections 3.9.3 and 6.4) and financial resources are also required.

The key informants at federal and regional levels stressed that there is an insufficient number of experts to service the ever-increasing number of agricultural projects. This, compounded with the absence of transportation, deters regular monitoring of the performance of the projects (LAD, Pers., Fed., 2014; EIAT, Pers., Fed., 2014; LUAU, Pers., Reg., 2014). One of the key informants said,

> The shortage of human resources is due partly to the investment promotion agencies' salary and benefits packages which are not as attractive as private sector remuneration. Hence, it is difficult for the agencies to fill vacant posts.

For instance, our agency has vehicles and funds for running costs such as petrol, but it doesn't have drivers to regularly monitor progress and provide support to the agricultural projects which are located in remote areas. Multiple driver posts have been advertised but it could not be filled.

(LAD, Pers., Fed., 2014)

The shortage of human resources, expertise and transportation in FDI promotion institutions at all levels of government results in deterring the timely and regular monitoring of the performance of all investment projects. In addition, the appropriate actions, including the provision of support to facilitate project implementation, cannot be taken in a timely manner.

The lack of technical capacity in these institutions, especially the EAILAA, can result in the provision of land that is not suitable for agricultural activities and the type of crops desired by the foreign investor (see Section 7.3.1). It can also lead to the setting of irrational lease prices, which are not based on an economic valuation of the land. Contracts that are not adequate and miss vital clauses are drafted, and opportunities for ensuring environmentally sustainable and pro-poor investments can thus be lost (see Sections 3.7 and 6.4).

The absence of institutional resources impedes the evaluation of the track record of investors to ascertain their motives (i.e. speculative versus long-term investors) and previous social and environmental performance to understand their potential in bringing the desired agricultural development prior to granting FDI rights. It is possible that investment permits for large-scale agriculture are given to investors who neither have experience in large-scale agriculture nor have a policy on corporate social and environmental responsibilities. It is to be noted that all the large-scale agricultural investors included in this study (see Section 7.3.1) do not have prior experience in large-scale agriculture, neither do they have an Environmental Management Unit (EMU) or an expert on environmental management and social affairs to ensure environmentally and socially mindful investments (see Sections 3.5 and 3.7).

The major problems related to the case study projects included the following:

1   **Delays in providing agricultural land:** There are delays in providing land after the issuance of investment permit. This is due to the inventory on available lands in the specific region not being accurate. There are no up-to-date land statistics (IPST, Pers., Fed., 2014; LAUD, Pers., Fed., 2014). One of the key informants said, "[A]t times, the registered available lands are occupied by smallholder farmers. Investors have to wait until the farmers are evacuated which could take more than a year. There are documented cases where investors received lands after two years" (IPST, Pers., Fed., 2014).

2   **Unsuitable land and location for agriculture:** Investors leased unsuitable lands for agricultural practices (i.e. flooding – see Sections 7.3.1), and lands were in unsuitable locations for the type of agricultural crops (i.e. prolonged rain – see Section 8.4). This has negatively affected agricultural project performance and caused financial loss (KAPP-SM, Pers., FIC, 2014; TAIP2-SM, Pers., FIC, 2014).

3   **Shortage of government services:** The Gambella and Beneshangul-Gumuz Regional States, where large-scale agricultural investments are encouraged, are severely short of government-provided services such as roads, electricity, telephone and Internet networks and banks (see Sections 7.2.1 and 7.2.2). The absence of these services contributes to the low performance of the agricultural projects and causes additional business costs (see Section 8.0). For instance, the absence of electric power deters the intensification of the agricultural project operations. Hence, they are forced to use diesel-based generators, which cause additional cost to the projects (see Section 7.3.1; KAPP-SM, Pers., FIC, 2014; TAIP2-SM, Pers., FIC, 2014; RAP-SM, Pers., FIC, 2014).

4   **Unavailability of a skilled workforce and high turnover of employees:** There are intertwined labour-related challenges surrounding the large-scale agricultural investments. The unavailability of local skilled workforce leads to the use of foreign workers who are costly compared to locals. This is not cost-effective for the projects (ESPD, Pers., Fed., 2014). The harsh environment[15] in which these investments are taking place leads to the high turnover of these workers (TAIP-SM2, Pers., FIC, 2014). This results in the projects hiring replacement foreign workers and processing work permits, which requires a lot of resources such as time and money (TAIP-SM2, Pers., FIC, 2014). The other challenge the investors face is the strictness of the Ethiopian labour law that does not allow hiring and firing as and when the projects need to do so. In the investors' opinion, this impairs efficient project operation (SESP-SM, Pers., FIC, 2014).

5   **Security issues:** The large-scale agricultural investors, especially in Gambella Regional State, have faced huge security problems (see Section 7.2.1). These contribute to the low performance of the projects and entail additional costs to the projects (SADP-SM1, Pers., FIC, 2014; SADP-SM2, Pers., FIC, 2014; RAP-SM, Pers., FIC, 2014; TAIP-SM2, Pers., FIC, 2014). All foreign agricultural projects are guarded by a large number of militia (the number is determined by the farm size and the level of security threat) that are provided by the government (TAIP-SM2, Pers., FIC, 2014). The agricultural projects provide fully equipped shelters as well as a monthly fee of an average Ethiopian birr 10,000 (about US$500) in addition to the farm guards hired by the projects (TAIP-SM2, Pers., FIC, 2014). This security threat results in these projects spending a lot of money so as to secure the farm sites. It also negatively affects the project operations (SADP-SM1, Pers., FIC, 2014; SADP-SM2, Pers., FIC, 2014; RAP-SM, Pers., FIC, 2014; TAIP-SM1, Pers., FIC, 2014, TAIP-SM2, Pers., FIC, 2014).

6   **Customs office lengthy processes:** The large-scale agricultural projects have difficulties in getting the imported agricultural inputs in a timely manner due to the lengthy processes of the Customs Office. This hampers the operations of the farms and incurs additional operational expenses to the projects (RAP-SM, Pers., FIC, 2014).

7 **Lack of coordination among government agencies:** The coordination problem among various sectors is obvious from the inadequate implementation of the investment policy. For instance, the absence of an adequate information exchange system among FDI promotion agencies at federal, regional and district levels results in taking contradictory decisions that cause an interruption in project operations and unnecessary loss of productivity. The Ruchi Agri PLC is a case in point. The company was given a four-year grace period for the land rent which was stated in the contract. The contract was signed with the EAILAA at the federal level. The district office was continuously asking the project to settle the annual lease payment despite that the project referred to the contract and refused to pay the requested payment. The district officials went ahead and stopped the project operations for 45 days until the problem was resolved (RAP-SM, Pers., FIC, 2014). This caused additional expenses, as well as delays in the project implementation (RAP-SM, Pers., FIC, 2014). This could be due to inadequate vertical information flow owing to the power relations between the various levels of government.

8 **Unrealistic decisions:** The lowland areas, where the large-scale agricultural investments are encouraged, are covered by forests, woodland and savanna land (see Sections 7.2 and 7.3.1). The investment projects had to clear the forests in order to develop the land. The government made a decision to give the wood from these forests to the local communities who neither have the right tools to work on these vast number of trees nor the vehicles to transport the felled trunks. The decision-makers are very much aware of the lack of capacity of the local communities, but the decision was made without designing a mechanism to assist them. The decision has some elements of community concern, but they were not fully executable and were not facilitated by the investment projects. For instance, the S&P Energy Solution PLC was instructed to give the wood to the community, and since the operation of moving large quantities of felled trees is beyond the community's capacity, these are lying on the farm site, resulting in termite infestation, and have become a wasted resource (SESP-SM, Pers., FIC, 2014).

6.6 Summary

Since its adoption of the ADLI strategy, the current government of Ethiopia has set in place a number of policies and institutions that are meant to attract inward FDI in large-scale agriculture and facilitate its operation. The main of those is the Investment Policy, the essences of which have been mainstreamed in the different sectoral policies, strategies and plans, such as the Rural Development Policy and Strategy, the Rural Land Administration and Land Use Policy, the Education and Training Policy, the Health Policy and Strategies, Infrastructure Development Policy, Labour Proclamation, Environmental Policy, Social Protection Policy and Growth and Transformation Plans. The government has also set up institutional and regulatory frameworks, the main ones of which are the EIC, the EAILAA and the Development Bank of Ethiopia.

The Agricultural Land Lease Agreements are the vital elements in ensuring the adequate implementation of the policies that are designed to promote agricultural and rural development in Ethiopia. However, the Land Lease Agreement format is very loose due mainly to the responsible agencies insufficient knowledge and experience in formulating contract of this nature. There are also other practical challenges, including lack of financial and human resources as well as expertise with the agencies implementing the investment policy. These challenges are compounded with the absence of infrastructure, such as electricity and roads, that further deter the facilitation of the operation. Hence, the implementation of the policies that are meant to support FDI in large-scale agriculture is inadequate.

Notes

1 The steps/phases are from subsistence (small scale) to diversified family agriculture (medium scale) to specialised commercial farming (large scale).
2 See studies by Timmer (1988), Todaro (2000) and Tsakok (2011) on agricultural transformation of Western nations.
3 The tax exemption includes income tax, import tax and export tax.
4 Health Extension Programme, which is based on expansion and construction of health facilities and developing Health Extension Workers, was designed to ensure the delivery of basic preventive and curative health services to the rural population.
5 Environment-related issues include natural resources, ecosystem biodiversity, energy resources, mineral resources, human settlement, pollution, tenure and access rights to land and natural resources, environmental information system, environmental research and environmental education and awareness.
6 Citizens' fundamental rights promote not only environmental sustainability but also pro-poor FDI in agriculture as they advocate for full participation in the planning and implementation of policies, programmes and projects such as agricultural investments affecting citizens directly.
7 Article 43 The Right to Development – 1. The Peoples of Ethiopia as a whole, and each Nation, Nationality and People in Ethiopia in particular have the right to improved living standards and to sustainable development. 2. Nationals have the right to participate in national development and, in particular, to be consulted with respect to policies and projects affecting their community. 3. All international agreements and relations concluded, established or conducted by the State shall protect and ensure Ethiopia's right to sustainable development. 4. The basic aim of development activities shall be to enhance the capacity of citizens for development and to meet their basic needs.
8 Article 44 Environmental Rights – 1. All persons have the right to a clean and healthy environment. 2. All persons who have been displaced or whose livelihoods have been adversely affected as a result of State programmes have the right to commensurate monetary or alternative means of compensation, including relocation with adequate State assistance
9 Article 92: Environmental Objectives – 1. Government shall endeavour to ensure that all Ethiopians live in a clean and healthy environment. 2. The design and implementation of programmes and projects of development shall not damage or destroy the environment. 3. People have the right to full consultation and to the expression of views in the planning and implementation of environmental policies and projects that affect them directly. 4. Government and citizens shall have the duty to protect the environment.
10 Before the establishment of the Investment Commission, investment related matters were handled by Ethiopian Investment Agency under Ministry of Industry.

11 Before the establishment of this agency, large-scale agricultural investment related matters were handled by Agricultural Investment Support Directorate under the Ministry of Agriculture.
12 The bank was established in 1909 and is a state-owned development finance institution.
13 These are codes of the interviewees, and the coding was deemed important to protect the sources as the issues of discussion are sensitive. See Appendix 1 for those codes and their referents.
14 Kebele is the lowest level of government at village level.
15 The lowland areas are very remote, have high risk of malaria and very hot weather; at times the temperature reaches more than 45 °C. There is no infrastructure such as clean water, electricity, roads or communication.

7 Description of the case study projects and the communities

7.1 Introduction

This chapter starts by providing a description of the profile of the Gambella and Beneshangul-Gumuz Regional States of Ethiopia where the case study projects are located. The FDI in large-scale agriculture is concentrated in these regions but mainly in Gambella (see Figure 7.1). Following this, the chapter describes the six foreign large-scale agricultural investment projects, chosen as the case studies for this book, as well as the communities in the surrounding areas of those projects. Five of them are located in Gambella Regional State, while one of them is situated in Beneshangul-Gumuz Regional State. These foreign investment projects leased a total of 218,000 hectares of land for cotton, soya bean, sugarcane, rice, palm and biofuel tree production (see Figure 7.2).

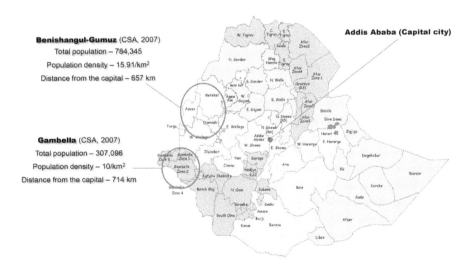

Figure 7.1 Locations of the Case Study Regions in Ethiopia
Source: Data from CSA (2007).

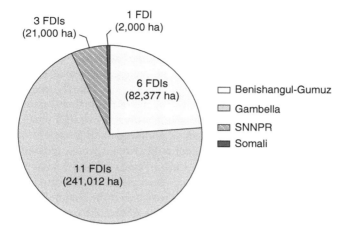

3 FDIs
(21,000 ha)

1 FDI
(2,000 ha)

6 FDIs
(82,377 ha)

☐ Benishangul-Gumuz
☐ Gambella
▨ SNNPR
■ Somali

11 FDIs
(241,012 ha)

Figure 7.2 Total Number of Foreign Investors in Large-Scale Agriculture and Total Size of Agricultural Land Leased to Foreigners in Ethiopia as of December 2014

7.2 Profiles of Gambella and Beneshangul-Gumuz Regions

FDI in large-scale agriculture has become a common practice in many regions of Ethiopia, more notably in Gambella and Beneshangul-Gumuz Regional States, which are endowed with natural resources, such as dense forestland, rivers, grassland, fertile soil and precious minerals. These regions are known as emerging regions due to significant lag in their social and economic development compared to other regions in Ethiopia. They are mostly dominated by agro-pastoral communities. They suffer from chronic marginalisation in terms of social and economic infrastructure development. Many parts of these regions are not yet accessible by modern transportation and communication facilities (MoFED et al., 2007).

7.2.1 Gambella regional state

Gambella Regional State is found in the southwest of Ethiopia about 800 kilometres from the Ethiopian Capital, Addis Ababa (ETA, 2015). The region borders with the Republic of South Sudan. The total area of the region is 30,065 square kilometres, and the population is about 307,000. The average population density is around 10 people per square kilometre. This makes Gambella Regional State the most sparsely populated region in Ethiopia (HoA-REC/N, 2012). There are five indigenous ethnic groups, which compose 76% of the total population of the region. These groups are Agnwak (27%), Nuer (40%), Majanger (6%), Opo and Komo (3%), with their own distinct languages. The two main languages are Nure and Agnwak. The Nure are mainly pastoralists while the Agnwak are crop farmers. The remaining 24% of the population are non-indigenous people from other parts of Ethiopia (Balcha, 2007). The communities are dependent on natural resources for their livelihoods. Forests are used for hunting wild animals, honey is extracted from beehives, wood is harvested for tools and grass for homesteads, medicinal plants are harvested and rivers are used for fishing (Balcha, 2007).

The region is endowed with natural resources such as rivers, many kinds of woodlands, forests, savanna grasslands, permanent and seasonal wetlands, wild animals and fertile soil. It has five ecological zones, namely plain land, grassland, wetland, woodland and forestland. The major rivers that Gambella treasures include Baro, Gillo and Alwaro. Gambella's diverse wildlife makes the region unique. The Gambella National Park is endowed with a variety of fauna and flora. It shelters about twenty significant wild animal species, most of which have international importance, as well as various kinds of birds, some of which are endemic. Wild animals such as wild pig, deer, elephant, lion and cheetah can be found (Briggs, 2013). One of the region's treasures is the Gambella National Park, which is located 768 kilometres west of Addis Ababa, the capital city of Ethiopia. It was established as a protected area in 1973 to conserve a diverse assemblage of wildlife and unique habitats such as an endangered species of wetland antelopes (Briggs, 2013; WCO, Pers., Reg., 2014).

At the time of the data collection (December 2014), 70% of the FDI projects in large-scale agriculture were located in Gambella Regional State (see Figure 7.2). Most of these agricultural lands were claimed from the Gambella National Park and other protected areas, indigenous forests, woodlands and savannah grasslands (EPU, Pers., Reg., 2014; WCO, Pers., Reg., 2014; FRAPUU, Pers., Reg., 2014; SNRDPUU, Pers., Reg., 2014).

The Gambella region has a severe security problem. During the data collection for this research, for instance, there was a curfew, as well as checkpoints along the thoroughfares. The region also suffers from poor infrastructure such as roads. The majority of local people live in abject poverty. The average household income is Ethiopian birr 13 (about US$0.66) per day. Communities live below the poverty line as per the World Bank definition of extreme poverty "as average daily consumption of $1.25 or less and means living on the edge of subsistence" (World Bank, 2010, p. np).

7.2.2 Beneshangul-Gumuz regional state

Beneshangul-Gumuz Regional State is located in the northwest of Ethiopia about 1,250 kilometres from the Ethiopian Capital Addis Ababa (ETA, 2015). The region borders with Sudan. The total area of the region is 51,000 square kilometres, and the population is about 656,000. The population density varies between towns, with the highest being 92.3 and the lowest is 3.9 persons per square kilometre. It ranges from 1 to 13 persons per square kilometre and is sparsely populated (CSA, 2007).

The region has five indigenous ethnic groups, which compose 57% of the total population. These groups are Berta (26%), Gumuz (23%), Shinasha (7%), Mao (0.6%) and Komo (0.2%). The remaining 43% consist of non-indigenous groups from other parts of Ethiopia (Balcha, 2007). Major local economic activities are crop farming and cattle rearing. Locals also practice small-scale mining. The major agricultural products are millet, sorghum, coffee and mangoes. Their livelihood is dependent mainly on natural resources such as forests and woodlands for hunting wild animals, honey beehives and forage and wood production for construction and fuel (Shete, 2011).

The region is endowed with natural resources including dense forests, river basins, precious minerals such as gold, copper, zinc, base metal, gum, granite and marble (Shete, 2011). The two major river basins are Abay (Blue Nile) and Baro-Akobo. There are several small rivers, such as Dabus, Yabus, Dura, Julia and Beles. These river basins have huge potential to supply drinking water, to irrigate agricultural lands and to generate hydroelectric power. They are the major tributaries of the Blue Nile River. There is a diverse assemblage of wild animals including lion, cheetah, antelope, buffalo, warthog, bushbuck and duiker. Despite having these many wild animals, dense forests and woodlands, there is no reserved park (Assosa University, 2015; Shete, 2011).

At the time of data collection (December 2014), 24% of the FDI projects in large-scale agriculture were located in Beneshangul-Gumuz Regional State. The region thus has the second-highest concentration of FDI in large-scale agriculture in Ethiopia after the Gambella Regional State (see Figure 7.2). These agricultural lands have mainly been claimed from forestlands.

The region is suffering from food insecurity, extreme poverty and poor infrastructure as in the Gambella Regional State. Food insecurity is a major challenge and malnutrition is affecting the health of the communities. The annual average income is about Ethiopian birr 7,850 (about US$354). Local people earn less than US$1 per day, which is under the poverty line as the World Bank definition of extreme poverty.

7.3 Profile of the case study projects and surrounding communities

7.3.1 The case study projects

The case studies of this research are six foreign large-scale agricultural investment projects described below. Five of the projects are located in Gambella Regional State and one of them in Beneshangul-Gumuz Regional State (see Table 4.2).

The lands leased to all these projects were forestland, savanna grassland, rivers, wetlands such as the Duma wetland, which is an environmentally sensitive area and found in the Gambella region and woodlands that contained endangered indigenous tree species. Some portions of the lands leased to the Karuturi and Saudi Star projects were, for instance, from the wildlife protected areas of the Gambella National Park.

These projects' operations cleared the forest and savanna grasslands, which are the natural habitat for a number of species of flora and fauna. These projects are fully based on intensive irrigation, for which most of the companies constructed

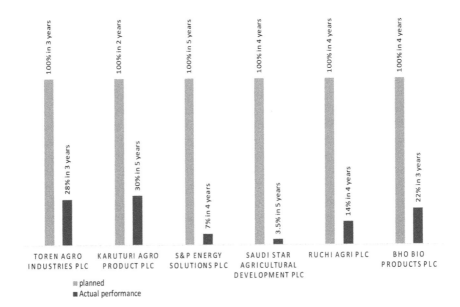

Figure 7.3 The Case Study Projects Planned Performance versus the Actual Performance in Producing the Agricultural Products

long irrigation canals, very long drainage system and storage ponds. For instance, Karuturi project constructed 120 km of a drainage system, 120 kilometres of dykes and about 50 kilometres of canals (KAPP-SM, Pers, FIC., 2014) for its operation, though many of these are structurally defective (IOM, 2014; Yassin, 2014). The performances of the projects are generally not as envisaged. Figure 7.3 shows these projects planned performance against actual performance.

7.3.1.1 Economic performance

The case study projects' economic performance in terms of production, exporting and foreign currency generation for the host country was very low due to various reasons, such as investors' being inexperienced in large-scale agriculture, weaknesses of local institutions that are mandated to facilitate FDI, as well as the ongoing security problem in these areas, absence of infrastructure such as electricity and road limit the intensification of the projects' operations.

As a result, the anticipated economic gain from these investments was not realised as their performance in developing the agricultural land was very low. For instance, the SN&P Energy Solution project aiming at producing biofuel in the region, which suffers from food insecurity, malnutrition and extreme poverty, has developed 7% of the land instead of 80% at the time this research was conducted in 2014. The BHO project, which was expected to develop 100% of the agricultural land within three years, has developed only 22% during the four years. Another extreme example is the Saudi Star project, which has developed only 3.5% of the agricultural land after five years, despite it was expected to develop 100% of the agricultural land within four years.

Furthermore, these projects agricultural production is very limited. For instance, the Ruchi project developed 3500 hectares of land out of the available 25,000 hectares and produced maize, soybeans and groundnuts. During the four years since the land was acquired, the project had developed only 14% of the agricultural land and produced 2 tonnes of groundnuts instead of the planned 8 tonnes and 375 tonnes of maize instead of the planned 750 tonnes (GRARDB, 2015). All the project's products are marketed locally (RAP-SM pers., FIC, 2014). This is despite the fact that the Ethiopian government's main objective for encouraging FDI in large-scale farming is to produce export-oriented products in order to increase its foreign earnings.

7.3.1.2 Employment creation and social responsibility

Again, their employment creation and wage rates for locals are generally low despite the stipulations in the national policy frameworks, such as the Rural Development Policy and Strategies (MoFED, 2003), which encourage the promotion of labour-intensive technology to adequately employ the abundant labour. All the projects are highly mechanised instead of labour-intensive; hence, employment creation for the abundant labour is low and seasonal. For instance, the Ruchi project's employees consisted of 11 Indians, who are in managerial, human resources, finance and engineering positions, and one Ethiopian, who supervises the local employees that are engaged in jobs operating farm machines as well as seasonal workers numbering about 200 per day in pick season and 35 per day at low season (RAP-SM, Pers., FIC, 2014). The Saudi Star project had created jobs for about 800 employees, including five foreigners. Of those employees, 185 were fixed-term experts and machine operators while the rest were seasonal labourers at the farm and the factory.[1] The Karuturi project created 55 fixed and 27 temporary jobs for Ethiopians in 2014 (GRARDB, 2015).

All the agricultural projects, except Toren, had wage rates that are below the standard rate in the sector. For instance, the rates are between Ethiopian birr 25 and 35 (i.e. about US$1.20–1.70) per day while the standard rate was Ethiopian birr 50.00 (about US$2.52). They didn't also offer insurance for medical expenses and long-term disabilities due to injuries while on the job or a pension. Besides the aforementioned limitations, most of these projects did not provide adequate accommodation for labourers, who came from other parts of Ethiopia and cannot commute every day like the workers from the surrounding community. For instance, the Ruchi project had only 10 huts. Most of the farms, such as Karuturi and BHO, did not provide a resting place for the labourers.

Some of the projects did not have direct labour agreement with the labourers. For instance, evidence from the EAILAA's environmental and social audit report of the Ruchi agricultural project reveals that the project does not have a direct labour agreement with the labourers who are instead employed by a third party. Hence, the labour agreement is made between the company and the third party. The farm administration rules and regulations are not yet established. The rights and responsibilities of workers are not clearly stated (EAILAA, 2014). This is in breach of the Ethiopian Labour Proclamation No. 377/2003, Article 4, Sub Articles 3 and 5 which state that

> a contract of employment should specify type of employment, place of work, the rate of wages, method of calculation thereof, manner and interval of payment and duration of the contract, as well as a contract of employment to adhere to the employment conditions provided by law, collective agreement or work rule.

These projects do not have a self-regulatory mechanism (i.e. Corporate Social Responsibility Policy) in which they monitor and prevent their projects' negative impact on the society. For instance, three adjacent villages (namely Bildak, Knjikocho and Pino) of the Karuturi farm were flooded during a rainy season in 2014 due mainly to the project's construction of water blockage dykes and the creation of dams to divert the Baro River's natural flow (ILICO, ILICO, Foc., 2014; EPU, Pers., Reg., 2014). As a result, the villagers were displaced, and it was not possible for this study to conduct focus group discussion with the affected villagers. It is clear that extended flooding for more than three months can cause waterborne diseases and exacerbate the health situation of the flood-affected communities, especially children, women, elderly and people with disabilities. The Gambella region has neither the health infrastructure to respond to the disaster nor the capacity to quickly provide the basic necessities such as medicine, clean water and food to the displaced people.

7.3.1.3 Environmental performance and occupational health and safety standards

These projects' environmental performance is also very low. Their agricultural waste is dumped into the environment without treatment, as they do not have a waste treatment plant. After-use chemical containers are buried in the ground, which renders a high risk of soil and groundwater contamination. Furthermore, the method used to apply agricultural chemicals, such as pesticides, insecticides and herbicides is spraying (sprinkling). This method of application runs a high risk of missing the target areas and the possibility of polluting the air, the soil and the surface water and thereby affecting the surrounding communities' well-being, which is likely to be immense. There was no water management system, such as water recycling, so as to ensure the availability of good quality water at sufficient quantity for future generations. Although water is currently in abundance in the area, this may not be the case in the long run if it is not used in a sustainable manner. In addition, these projects have conducted the E&SIA report after the commencement of their operations, notwithstanding the Ethiopian Environmental Impact Assessment Proclamation (Proclamation. No. 299/2002), which demands projects to undertake an EIA before commencing the projects.

One of the recommendations of each project EIA report, for instance, is the establishment of an Environmental and Social Affairs Unit, so that the mitigation measures identified in this report can be implemented. Furthermore, this Unit ensures the implementation of Ethiopia's environmental and social related policies, regulation and directives, including the Environmental Code of Practice for Agricultural Investments, prepared by the Ministry of Agriculture in 2010. This Code of Practice for Agricultural Investment provides a mechanism to promote environmentally friendly agricultural practices including the protection of the health and safety of farmworkers and the community. This code of Practice is a minimum standard and a mandatory to all farms. For example, the E&SIA report of the Karuturi project affirmed that the project could only be feasible if the project implements the Socio-economic Impact Management Plan (SIMP) of the study without delay. If the SIMP was implemented in good time, it could have resolved the socio-economic problems that arose in the project area such as flooding (CMCD, Pers., Fed., 2014; EPU, Pers., Reg., 2014). For instance, the project's E&SIA study report was published in July 2011, but the project had not taken any of the mitigation measures described in the report until November 2014.[2] The report reveals that the estimated monetary value of the savanna grass, used for grazing by local pastoralists, and the indigenous trees, which the project began removing, amount to Ethiopian birr 813,000,000.00 (about US$47.4 million)[3] and Ethiopian birr 350,000,000.00 (US$20.4 million), respectively (Karuturi Agro-product PLC E&SI Report 2011).

The two critical documents, which have significant importance to ensure the minimisation of the adverse impacts of the projects on the environment, are absent from the farm sites. These documents are EIA report of the projects, which should include an action plan for the mitigation measures of significant social and environmental risks of the projects, and the Ethiopian Environmental Code of Practice for agricultural investment. These documents should have been working manuals for the agricultural workers, especially the farm managers.

These projects do not have an appropriate place to store agrochemicals, such as fertilisers and pesticides. All the various types of chemicals are stored together without categorising them by name and the composition of their active ingredients. This is a potential chemical hazard for the environment and the communities surrounding these projects. Handling chemicals by agricultural workers is another area of concern. For example, the agricultural workers handle agrochemicals, such as fertilisers and pesticides without protective equipment, clothing and other materials. These entail a huge risk of occupational safety and health of these workers. Similarly, the Saudi Star rice-husking factory workers did not have approved industry-standard safety gear (i.e. protective equipment) to protect them from occupational hazards (SADP-FW, Pers. FIC, 2014). The practice is a breach of all Ethiopian laws that provide occupational health and safety of agricultural workers, particularly the Ethiopian Labour Proclamation no. 377/2003, Article

92, which obliges employers to comply with the occupational safety, health and working environment requirements, and Article 12, which specifies employers' obligations in addition to the special stipulations in the contract of employment. It is also a violation of the signed investment agreements.

7.3.1.4 Technology transfer and creation of 'out-grower schemes'

The national investment policy frameworks further stress the promotion of labour-intensive technology to adequately use the abundant labour, upgrading the skills of agricultural workers and the creation of direct linkages between agricultural investors and local smallholder farmers through "out-grower scheme". However, the government has not put in place mechanisms to ensure that these investments in large-scale agriculture transfer the required technology and know-how to the local people, especially those of smallholder farmers, and increase FDI spillover effect. These investment projects are highly mechanised, and it's impossible for the smallholder farmers, who apply primitive tools and are not adequately capacitated, to take up high-tech farming methods.

Furthermore, the agricultural lease agreements of these projects, which are legally binding document, don't encourage the creation of linkages with local smallholder farmers despite the investment policy advocates for it. This could pave ways to upgrade the smallholders farming method and increase their productivity. This, in turn, ensures for the smallholder farmers food sufficiency and additional income generation.

7.3.2 The case study communities

The case study projects are adjacent to six communities. The communities pursue different livelihood activities, mainly farming, livestock rearing, fishery and bee-keeping (see Table 7.1).

These communities use very primitive tools (i.e. hoe and hand tools) to cultivate crops, and the harvest is not sufficient to satisfy their families' food need throughout the year. The forests were a sacred place and ancestral burial sites for the communities as well as a source of livelihoods providing extra food sources during the dry season and food shortages. Hence, their livelihoods were dependent on the surrounding natural resources such as forests and rivers. For example, they were using the areas outside the forest fringes for cultivating maize, sorghum and groundnuts and the rivers, where they practise fishing to sustain the family food security and generate income by selling the surplus product (PUKCO, FOC., 2014).

The agricultural projects neither created jobs for the communities nor transferred technologies to the local communities. They didn't even provide support to upgrade the communities' farming tools in order to increase production and secure food to compensate for the loss of their forestlands. Furthermore, the loss of local land rights and indigenous land-use practices have a significant negative impact on the communities' well-being as well as the ecology (Moreda, 2013). For example, the Karuturi agricultural project constructed a water blockage system

Name of Community/district	Community's regional state	Community's ethnic group	Description of the surrounding	Community's major livelihoods	Adjacent agricultural investment project	Type of agricultural investment	Community's participation in the negotiation of the agricultural investment project
Dangur and Guba	Beneshangul-Gumuz	Gumuz	Forestland and rivers	Livestock rearing, crop production and honey production	ShaPorji (S&P) Energy Solution	Biofuel trees (Pongamia) and edible oil crops	Neither the community nor the regional administrative bureau knew about the deal which took place between the federal government and the investor
Illia	Gambella	Agnuwak	Woodland, savanna grassland and rivers	Crop farmers	Karuturi	Palm, cereals and pulses	The community was not consulted about the agricultural project beforehand. They came to know when the project started cutting the trees and savanna grasses and building its camp.
Pukedi	Gambella	Agnuwak	Forestland and rivers	Crop farmers	Saudi Star	Rice	These communities were not consulted about the leasing of the forestland for commercial farming. The villagers came to know only when the project started clearing the forestland which they claim as their ancestral land.
Perbengo	Gambella	Agnuwak	Forestland and rivers	Crop farmers	Saudi Star	Rice	
Wathgac	Gambella	Nure	Savanna grassland and rivers	Livestock rearing, fishing and crop farming	BHO	Cereal, pulses and edible oil crops	The community was informed after the deal was done between the government and the investor.
Ulleng/ Pugnido	Gambella	Agnuwak	Forestland (mainly shea trees) and woodland	Crop farming	Ruchi Toren	Edible oil crops Cotton and soybean	The community did not have prior information about the projects. They came to know about it when the investors started deploying the farm machinery and felling the trees.

and created dams to divert the Baro River's natural flow to irrigate its cultivation. This causes the river to overflow, especially during the rainy season, and resulted in flooding which negatively impacted the farm site, the adjacent communities and the environment.

It is clear that extended flood for more than three months can cause waterborne diseases and exacerbate the health situation of the flood-affected communities, especially children, women, elderly and people with disabilities. The region has neither the health infrastructure to respond to the disaster nor the capacity to quickly provide the basic necessities such as medicine, clean water and food to the displaced people. The economic and social impact of the floods might be significant and requires further study that is beyond the scope of this study.

7.4 Summary

The six case study projects covered by this study are located in Gambella and Beneshangul-Gumuz Regional States of Ethiopia, which are endowed with natural resources, such as dense forestland, rivers, grassland, fertile soil and precious minerals. Five of the projects are located in the Gambella region and one in Beneshangul-Gumuz. Each project has claimed from a minimum of 6,000 hectares to a 100,000 hectares of virgin land, at the initial stages but with the possibility to lease many more acres of fertile lands. Four of the projects are Indian companies, one is Saudi Arabian and the other one is a Turkish company. Most of these agricultural lands were claimed from the national park and other protected areas, indigenous forests, woodlands and savanna grasslands.

The projects affect negatively a number of communities from different ethnic groups in the areas adjacent to the projects. These projects' have poorly performed in contributing to the Ethiopian economic growth, employment creation, technology transfer and environmental and social protection.

Notes

1 The Saudi Star project was established to produce rice, and it has a rice-husking factory adjacent to the farm in Gambella.
2 November 2014 was the time these data were collected in Gambella Regional State.
3 The Ethiopian birr depreciated more than 100% against the US dollar between 2008 and 2014. The depreciation has been gradual; that is US$1 was about Ethiopian birr 9.00 in 2008, 13 in 2010, 16 in 2011, 18 in 2013 and 20 in 2014.

8 Analysis and reflection

8.1 Introduction

This section presents the results of the analysis of the case studies described in Section 7.3. The analysis is guided by the frameworks that were established in Sections 3.7 (pro-poor and sustainable FDI in agriculture, and fundamental principles of pro-poor and sustainable investment in agriculture) and 3.8 (frameworks and guidelines to assess investment policies). It is further informed by the theoretical foundation that was discussed in Section 1.3.1. In addition, the performance of each case study project in terms of the protection of the environment and their contribution to social and economic development was analyzed based on the pro-poor and environmentally sustainable investment criteria (see Table 8.1 and Appendix 4). Following the analysis of each case study, a cross-case analysis of the six case studies was undertaken.

Finally, evidence from each case study is triangulated to draw common conclusions on the effects of FDI in large-scale agriculture in Ethiopia (see Figure 8.1). Relevant findings of previous research on the subject matter were also used to deepen the analysis concerning the practical support of the Ethiopian Investment Policy for FDI in large-scale agriculture to be pro-poor and environmentally sustainable (see Sections 3.9.3 and 6.2.3).

8.2 Analysis of the case studies and their results

The performance of each case study project was evaluated using the assessment criteria for pro-poor and environmentally sustainable investment. A five-level rating system ranging from very good to poor was used to assess each case study separately. The numerical scores were assigned on a normative basis to the performance of each case study in each criterion. These criteria encompass good governance focusing particularly on poverty reduction, human development, productive employment, social integration and environmental protection. These include aspects such as community participation in the negotiation of the agricultural land lease, improvements of local population food security, local population benefits from the investment, quantification of the agricultural project's environmental

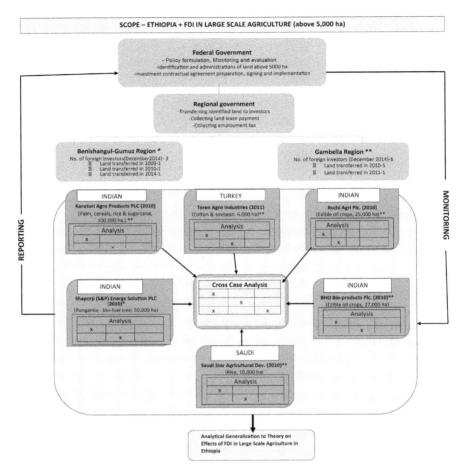

Figure 8.1 Cross-Case Analysis and Analytical Generalisation to Theory on the Effects of FDI in Large-Scale Agriculture in Ethiopia

impacts, managing agricultural waste and advocating for the sustainable use of resources (see Sections 3.7 and 3.8).

The data, collected from various sources, is graded on performance assessment rating system as follows: 1 = poor, 2 = fair, 3 = average, 4 = good, 5 = very good. Detailed scoring of each of the criterion for each case study is given in Appendix 4. Table 8.1 shows each case study project's performance and their total score.

Assessment of Agricultural Investment Projects Against Pro-Poor and Environmentally Sustainable Investment Criteria

Pro-poor investment criteria	Case study project					
	Karuturi	Saudi Star	Ruchi	Toren	BHO	S&P[1]
Existing rights to natural resources are recognised and respected	1	1	1	1	1	1
Participation of local residents, especially indigenous people, in the negotiation of large-scale land lease	1	1	1	1	1	1
Improvement of local farmers' farming methods	1	1	1	1	1	1
Improvements of local population's food security	1	1	1	1	1	1
Creation of jobs for local population	3	2	1	4	1	NA
Agricultural products (i.e. staple[2] vs non-staple; food crops vs industrial crops[3])	2	1	2	3	2	1
Respecting the core labour standards including wages, working hours, health insurance, occupational health and safety and other benefits	2	2	1	5	1	NA
Labour-intensive technology is used to create more jobs for the locals	1	1	1	1	1	1
Out-grower scheme is practised (i.e. creation of direct linkage between the project and local smallholder farmers)	1	1	1	1	1	1
Support to improve the local community's road, schools and health centres (i.e. Corporate Social Responsibility)	3	1	1	4	1	NA
Total Score = 50	**16**	**12**	**11**	**22**	**11**	**7**
Environmentally sustainable investment criteria						
Environmental impacts of the project are quantified	2	2	1	2	2	1
Measures taken to mitigate the negative impacts of the project	1	2	1	3	2	1
Measures taken to ensure sustainable use of resources	1	1	1	1	1	1
Agricultural waste is managed as per industry best practice	1	1	1	4	1	NA
Agrochemicals are managed as per Environmental Code of Practice for Agricultural investment	1	1	1	4	1	NA
Total Score = 25	**6**	**7**	**5**	**14**	**6**	**3**
Grand Total Score: 50 + 25 = 75	**22**	**19**	**16**	**36**	**17**	**10**
Grand Total Score for S&P: 35 + 15 = 50						

[1] S&P: This study was not able to make a direct observation on the farm site and its surroundings. Hence, three of the pro-poor criteria cannot be assessed (i.e. 15 points) and two of the environmentally sustainable criteria (i.e. 10 points) cannot be assessed. For the remaining criteria (50 points), the data were gathered from the preliminary discussion with the representative (see Appendix 1) as well as from various documents on the environmental and social performance assessment of the project (see Appendix 3).The potential total score for assessing pro-poor and environmentally sustainable large-scale agricultural investment is 75, except for the S&P agricultural project to which the potential total score is 50 as five of the criteria are not applicable as access to the farm site was denied.

[2] Case study areas' staple foods are maize, sorghum and millet. Toren Agro PLC scored the highest with a score of 36 while Karuturi, Saudi Star, BHO, Ruchi and S&P scored very low. It is evident that these large-scale agricultural investments do not encourage pro-poor and environmentally sustainable investment as they all scored less than 50% of the total score.

[3] Industrial crops are crops that provide material inputs for industrial processes and products such as oil crops, textile crops and biofuel crops. Its production potentially competes with food crops for land, water and other factors of production. The end product might not be available for the local population. The results of the assessment are shown in Figure 8.2 for each assessed agricultural project. A summary graph is also used to show the overall assessment of these agricultural investment projects (see Figure 8.3).

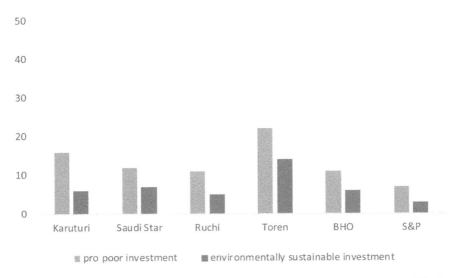

Figure 8.2 Total Score of Each Agricultural Project's Performance on Pro-Poor and Environmentally Sustainable Investment

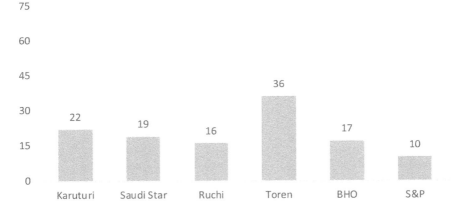

Figure 8.3 Overall Score of Each Agricultural Project's Performance on Pro-Poor and Environmentally Sustainable Investment

8.3 Discussion of the results

The implementation and outcome of the case study projects are analyzed from the perspective of the three pillars of sustainable development (i.e. social, environmental and economic) that are fundamental for promoting inclusive and green growth which many African countries, including Ethiopia, have been striving to achieve.

There are three main players with different interests that affect, or are affected by, the implementation of the case study projects. These players are the Ethiopian government and the foreign investors who have an influence on the implementation and hence on the outcome of the agricultural projects, while the communities of the project areas are affected either positively or negatively.

The following subsections present the discussion on the performance of the agricultural projects and the critical reflections, focusing on the three dimensions of sustainable development (economic, social and environment). It also draws lessons.

8.3.1 The projects' contribution to economic growth

The Ethiopian government attempts to attract FDI through the provisions of investment incentives, guarantees and protection and remittance of funds. The incentives include tax exemptions (income, import and export), long-term loans with very low interest rates, the ability to lease large tracts of land for half a century with very low lease prices and four- to five-year grace periods. These generous investment incentives are granted up front without sufficient conditions in favour of Ethiopia and its citizens.

Furthermore, the information requested in the investment permit application form is general and does not have local content requirements and does not seek information that could allow distinguishing between speculative and long-term investors. It also does not have aspects of investors' previous experience in the requested investment project as well as investors' track records in economic, social and environmental performance. Once a foreign investor allocates the minimum capital requirement (US$200,000) for an investment project, the said entity is granted the investment permit and the incentives immediately.

The envisaged investment benefits from these case study projects are not materialised. The benefits include skills upgrading of agricultural workers through training, creating linkages between foreign investors and local smallholder farmers through an "out-grower scheme" and producing export-oriented agricultural products in order to boost export which in turn increases Ethiopia's foreign earnings.

8.3.2 The projects' contribution to inclusive growth

The Ethiopian investment policy advocates for pro-poor investment. It encourages pro-poor FDI in large-scale agriculture, specifically in the case studies areas, which require a significant amount of development. However, the agricultural projects' contribution to creating jobs for as well as transferring knowledge to local residents are very limited. For instance, there was no training provided for the locals to upgrade their skills and offer them better and enduring jobs rather than seasonal and unskilled manual jobs. In addition, the projects did not create linkages between foreign investors and local smallholder farmers through an "out-grower scheme". It fails to comply with industry-standard safety protection measures for the local workers while on duty as per the Ethiopian Occupational Safety, Health, and Working Environment Proclamation No. 377/2003, Article 92. The majority of the projects' labour wage rate are lower than the industry wage standard.

Moreover, the lands that were leased for commercial farming was forestlands which were the communities' livelihoods such as food security, income generation and ritual places. For instance, during the dry season and when there was a shortage of food, the communities used to use the forestlands to collect stem plants and hunt wild animals for food. The forestlands are not only their food security; it is also their income generation through producing honey, harvesting medicinal plants and collecting firewood for selling. The forestlands have important historical, cultural and spiritual meanings for the communities, especially for the indigenous people who have a distinct spiritual relationship with their lands.

The communities are crop farmers, pastoralists and fishers. The projects not only claimed their forestlands but also their rivers for irrigation. The long canals and storage ponds constructed to irrigate water from the rivers created problems for the communities' cattle to pass to the grasslands. In addition, the projects extensive irrigation from the rivers will soon affect fish production, which is one of the resources of food and income for the communities.

8.3.3 The projects' contribution to environmental sustainability

The lands that were leased to the case study projects are either forestlands or savanna grasslands, all of which are surrounded by rivers that have sensitive wetlands. Some of the lands were claimed from Gambella National Park, which is a protected area and shelters quite a number of wild animals. The forestlands contained indigenous tree species that have endangered status.

The projects' operations cleared the forests and savanna grasses to develop the lands for cultivation. The forests, which are the natural habitat for a number of species of flora and fauna. Although the lease agreement stipulates to leave a windbreak of indigenous trees, this was never implemented. In addition, the projects use excessive water for irrigation and don't have in place a water management system, such as water recycling, so as to ensure the availability of quality water at sufficient quantity for future generations. Although water is currently in abundance in the project areas, this may not be the case in the long run if the resource is not used in a sustainable manner.

Furthermore, the projects do not have a waste management scheme such as a waste treatment plant. Agricultural waste was dumped into the environment without treatment and it has a huge negative impact on the soil and groundwater. The method used to apply agricultural chemicals, such as pesticides, is spraying.

This method of application runs a high risk of missing the target areas and the possibility of affecting the surrounding communities is likely to be immense. The farms do not have an appropriate place to store agrochemicals such as fertilisers and pesticides. They are stored in a metal container. In addition, all the various types of chemicals are stored together without categorising them by name and the composition of their active ingredients. This is a potential chemical hazard.

All these projects conducted the E&SIA of their respective projects after long they started operations despite the E&SIA Proclamation demands projects to carry out E&SIA before commencement in order to identify and mitigate significant negative impacts of the projects timely. Additionally, the project E&SIA report, which should include measures to mitigate the adverse impacts of the project, was not available at the farm although it should be used on site as an operational manual. For instance, one of the mitigation measures is the projects to establish an Environmental Management and Social Affairs Unit (EMSAU) in order to implement the rest of the mitigation measures for the adverse impact of the farm activities identified in the E&SIA report of the respective projects. Neither of the projects in this case study has an EMSAU nor an environmental expert.

The projects do not have a plan to offset their carbon footprints and promote sustainable agricultural practices. Hence, they affect the environment negatively, which, in turn, exacerbate the situation of climate change and the food insecurity of the local people.

8.4 Why these agricultural projects fail in all aspects

There are many reasons for these projects failure in contributing to the communities' well-being, environmental protection and economic growth. The majority of the foreign investors have neither prior experience in large-scale agriculture nor knowledge of the indigenous people culture and way of life. They are short-term profit speculative investors who saw the competitiveness of arable lands in light of the global food and financial crises in 2007 and 2008. Besides, the Ethiopian institutions that are responsible to facilitate these investments and enforce Ethiopian laws are very weak. This is evident from the absence of communities, who have local knowledge and could advise on the land suitability, during the identification of lands for commercial farming. This resulted in doing inadequate land-use planning and leasing ecologically sensitive areas, such as forestlands, woodlands, savanna grasslands, national parks, a wildlife sanctuary and sensitive wetlands that are not suitable for the practice of agriculture. This has a huge negative impact on the ecological and economic services of the flora and fauna in support of the local livelihoods.

Furthermore, the land lease agreements were signed by the investors and the government without including the communities in the contract negotiations. This land-lease agreement format is very loose in addressing the crucial and obvious social and environmental problems related to large-scale agriculture. It excludes essential clauses such as farm insurance to cover pollution and environmental liability, conservation plans, conditions of the farmland on return, arrangements for compensation, maintenance and repairing the farmland, security deposit, monitoring and reporting format and frequency, non-point source pollution, the number and type of jobs to be created for the locals and engagement with the local smallholder farmers to improve their farming methods. These lease agreements are one of the instruments to implement policies that are designed to promote agricultural and rural development in Ethiopia.

The institutions' weaknesses are also evident from the inadequate monitoring and reporting of the compliance of the lease agreements and Ethiopian laws, such as labour and environment, as well as sanctioning the non-compliance. For instance, E&SIAs of these projects were done long after the projects started operations, and that is a breach of the E&SIA Proclamation.

The agricultural projects predicament to the desired economic performance is that many folds. The investors' lack of experience in large-scale agriculture is compounded by the absence of government services such as roads, electricity and communications infrastructure. For instance, the absence of electric power deters the intensification of the farm operations. This, in turn, resulted in forcing the projects to use diesel-based generators, which cause additional cost to the projects. Besides, there is a severe security problem in the regions, especially Gambella due to the civil war in the Republic of South Sudan that created a cross-border conflict, communities' resistance to a huge influx of large-scale agricultural investment projects and ethnic conflicts between indigenous people and agricultural workers from other parts of Ethiopia.

These consequences are due mainly to rushed and unreasoned move by the government to promote investment in large-scale agriculture which is exacerbated by the absence of community participation in the decision-making process, and absence of PLUP and E&SIA which are effective tools to ensure environmental, economic and social sustainability.

The outcomes of these projects can, therefore, be considered failures for all stakeholders as follows:

- the communities: the projects portend significant negative implications for their well-being and the protection of the natural environment;
- the government: the performance of the projects is poor despite the government generous incentives to encourage agricultural investments, especially in the case study areas, with the view to expedite agricultural transformation to ensure food security for the country's growing population and to increase foreign earnings while responding to the global demand for agricultural products such as food and biofuel crops; and
- the investors: the absence of government services, such as electric power, better road and communication infrastructure, and social instability and deteriorated security situation caused the projects to delay implementation as well as to bear extra costs in order to ensure their operations such as security services, fuel to run diesel generators and ESAT Internet services.

8.5 Further reflections on the low performance of the large-scale agricultural projects

The low performance of the agricultural projects against the sustainability and pro-poor assessment criteria has many implications on the government (i.e. government institutions established to implement the investment policy; see Section 6.3). First and foremost, these institutions are mandated to facilitate the adequate implementation of the investment policy. These include ensuring community participation in the process of these agricultural investments such as LUP and the negotiation of the lease agreement. In addition, these institutions ensure the selection of potential investors and the provision of government services such as electric power, roads and communication so as to facilitate the operation of the project. However, these institutions are not capacitated with the required financial and human resources, such as knowledge and skills to adequately perform their mandates (see Sections 6.4 and 6.5). As a result, these agricultural investment projects failed to have positive impacts on economic, social and environmental development (see Appendix 4).

The investment process was conducted between the Federal government and investors without involving the communities. This is in breach of Article 92 of the Constitution (Proclamation No.1/1995), which states "citizens have the right to full consultation and to the expression of views in the planning and implementation of projects that affect them directly". In addition, it is in breach of the Environmental Policy (see Section 6.2.8) which ensures fundamental rights of all citizens that are enshrined in Articles 43[1] and 44[2] of the Constitution (Proclamation No.1/1995). The Environmental Policy advocates for community participation in all phases of environmental and resource development and management, the protection of cultural and natural heritage, LUP, EIA and SEA. The EIA Proclamation No. 299/2002, Article 15 stipulates public participation, especially for communities that are likely to be affected by the implementation of a project, in the preparation of the environmental impact study of the project. All the case study projects conducted E&SIA for their respective projects only after commencing operation. This is in breach of the EIA Proclamation. Second, the identified project risk mitigation measures were not yet implemented at the time of data collection. This shows that the E&SIA was prepared just to comply with the rules rather than to make a real impact on the ground.

The current Ethiopian land-lease agreements are inadequate to safeguard the environment and benefit the local communities (see Sections 6.4, 7.3.1. and 7.3.2). In addition, it is also inadequate as a tool to hold investors liable for the negative impact of projects on the environment and communities. The leased areas in the case studies included much land not suitable for farming. Forestlands, woodlands and savanna grasslands are included as well as national parks, a wildlife sanctuary and sensitive wetlands. The FDI projects cleared the trees and savanna grasses (see Section 7.3.1). This has a considerable negative impact on the ecosystem, including the economic services of the flora and fauna. This clearly shows the EAILAA's failure to identify major environmental problems related to large-scale agriculture and to address these in the lease agreements in a manner that is legally binding to ensure compensation for any damages (see Section 6.4). Furthermore, all the case study projects failed against the pro-poor and environmentally sustainable investment criteria (see Section 8.2). This low performance demonstrates the failure of both institutions (i.e. EIC and EAILAA) to verify the previous agricultural practices of the investors and their track records in promoting sustainable agricultural practices. This should be one of the criteria to give an investment permit so as to select potential investors.

The institutions, as well as the investors, failed in ensuring the fundamental rights of agricultural workers as discussed in Sections 3.7 and 3.8. All of the case study agricultural projects, except Toren, fail to respect the core labour standards (see Section 6.2.7 and Appendix 4). Hence, they pay very low wages, do not pay overtime, do not have insurance for occupational injuries and do not comply with the occupational health and safety standards in agriculture. These core labour standards are indicators of pro-poor FDI in agriculture. They are in accordance with the Ethiopian Constitution of Article 42 (Proclamation No. 1/1995) which states the rights of labour. The lack of adherence does not conform to the ILO's decent work agenda, which promotes employment creation, workers' rights, social protection and dialogue so as to achieve fair globalisation and the reduction of poverty. In addition, the case study agricultural projects are highly mechanised and consequently, they have not created many jobs (see Sections 7.3.1 and 7.3.2). This is in breach of the investment policy, which promotes labour-intensive technology with the view to create employment for the abundant labour (see Sections 6.2.1 and 6.2.10). These investments fail to create linkages with smallholder farmers. The continued use of primitive tools to cultivate agricultural land by local farmers is but one stark visual reminder of the lost opportunities for the upliftment of local communities (see Section 7.3.2).

These agricultural projects and the institutions failed to respect the human right to food as discussed in Table 3.1. Food insecurity for the local population is exacerbated since they are denied access to many natural resources that were part and parcel of the livelihoods of communities prior to the implementation of FDI projects (see Section 7.3.2). This compounds the current struggles for survival in local communities since the projects have not created enough jobs to compensate for lost livelihoods.

Revenue benefits to local communities are limited to the land lease payment, which is very low and does not cover the food needs of the local communities. Furthermore, the projects have a four- to five-year grace period to pay the lease. This implies that there is no immediate revenue to the communities. The performance of the projects is very low in terms of their production of agricultural products to contribute to the overall economic growth of Ethiopia (see Sections 6.5 and 7.3.1.1). This verifies that the incentives, which are not based on performance and are provided prior to investment, are a loss to Ethiopia (see Section 2.4.7). This practice undermines the Rural Development Policy which underscores the importance of foreign investments in large-scale agriculture to provide capital and agripreneurial skills that are required to facilitate agricultural transformation at the local level (see Section 6.2.1).

As described in Chapter 6, the government of Ethiopia has a good intent in promoting FDI in large-scale agriculture by putting in place adequate policy in FDI in agriculture so as to unleash the potential and strengthen Ethiopia's food security, improve livelihoods of the local community and safeguard the environment. However, the findings of this book demonstrate that these objectives are far from being achieved. This implies that the government of Ethiopia is in a difficult situation to achieve both objectives (i.e. economic growth while protecting the environment), and therefore, it has made a trade-off to attract investors who may be reluctant to invest in a country like Ethiopia that doesn't have adequate infrastructure (i.e. roads, electricity and water) and high-skilled labour to sufficiently facilitate the investments. Furthermore, the competition for the same investors from other African countries, which offer arable lands with low environmental standards and lax environmental regulations, is high. These probably make the government of Ethiopia refrain from enforcing stricter environmental and labour standards until it secures the required infrastructure and intrastructure that put the country in competitive and comparative advantages.

8.6 Summary

This chapter analyzed the results of the case study projects' performance against the features of pro-poor and environmentally sustainable FDI in large-scale agriculture and the fundamental principles to promote pro-poor and environmentally sustainable FDI in large-scale agriculture. Results of the cross-case analysis revealed that except Toren Agro PLC, the remaining five projects showed a generally low rating on overall performance in terms of environmental, social and economic development variables. Signs of inclusive growth were not witnessed in any of the projects, which were found to be rather low-paying to labourers (a practice tantamount to labour exploitation), not following labour standards and lacking occupational health and safety measures. Furthermore, technology transfer, which is one of the gains anticipated from those projects, was not witnessed by the findings of the study. Furthermore, the creation of out-grower schemes (links with to local smallholder farmers) has remained a remote target.

Although the Investment Policy supports pro-poor and environmentally sustainable investments in large-scale agriculture, essential elements, such as capable institutions are missing. The government and investors in those agricultural projects are shy in terms of delivering responsible agricultural investments that recognise and respect human rights and natural resources tenure rights of communities. The absence of government services, such as electric power and road and communications infrastructure, and unreliable security situations were practical challenges for those investors. The cumulative outcome renders the overall aim of the Investment Policy irrelevant, ineffective and inefficient and thus in need of credible efforts from the EIC to make large-scale agricultural projects pro-poor and environmentally sustainable to help effect the structural transformation of the economy.

Notes

1 Article 43 The Right to Development – 1) The Peoples of Ethiopia as a whole, and each Nation, Nationality and People in Ethiopia in particular have the right to improved living standards and to sustainable development. 2) Nationals have the right to participate in national development and, in particular, to be consulted with respect to policies and projects affecting their community. 3) All international agreements and relations concluded, established or conducted by the State shall protect and ensure Ethiopia's right to sustainable development. 4) The basic aim of development activities shall be to enhance the capacity of citizens for development and to meet their basic needs.

2 Article 44 Environmental Rights – 1) All persons have the right to a clean and healthy environment. 2) All persons who have been displaced or whose livelihoods have been adversely affected as a result of State programmes have the right to commensurate monetary or alternative means of compensation, including relocation with adequate State assistance.

9 Conclusions and recommendations

9.1 Conclusions

This book's investigation focuses on environmental, social and economic performance of FDI in large-scale agriculture in Ethiopia. It studies the Ethiopian investment policy and other relevant sectors' policies with regard to their support to promote pro-poor and environmentally sustainable FDI in large-scale agriculture.

The book provides historical account of FDI in large-scale agriculture in Ethiopia starting from imperial time to date in order to give a perspective of its' trend. It reveals that FDI in large-scale agriculture is not a new phenomenon in Ethiopia. It was already practised and encouraged during the time of Emperor Haile Selassie I (1930–74). During the military regime, FDI was halted and state-owned large-scale farms were promoted. FDI in agriculture was reinstated with the EPRDF government that took power in 1991 (see Chapter 4).

The current government's (EPRDF's) investment policy encourages FDI in large-scale agriculture, especially in sparsely populated lowland areas. The overall objective of the investment policy is to expedite agricultural transformation through large-scale commercial farming (see Section 6.2). However, despite a favourable policy environment, execution of FDI is inadequate. The lack of capacity within the institutions charged with promotion of FDI, along with inexperience of the foreign investors in large-scale agriculture, contributed to the lack of delivery (see Sections 6.5, 7.3 and 8.4). Most of the case study projects leased large-scale agricultural land in Ethiopia due to speculation after the 2007 global food crisis, as well as very low land-lease prices with generous incentives. These investors had been leasing large tracts of land for over five years at the time of data collection. Despite this, the development and production envisaged in the lease agreement have not been realised. These investments have failed against pro-poor, environmentally sustainable and economically viable assessment criteria (see Section 8.2). This proves that the Ethiopian-rising narrative is based on only GDP growth, and hence, it is incomplete as it overlooks inclusive and sustainable growth which are the two important elements of sustainable development.

Evidently, strong institutions are vital for realizing policy objectives. As discussed in Chapter 5, despite the Ethiopian government's good intentions and policies, FDI in large-scale agriculture are not as successful as they should be.

The investment policy needs to go a step further to ensure that the institutions promoting investment have sufficient capacity to plan and deliver as well as to monitor and enforce compliance in FDI. Only then will the policy objectives be realised (see Sections 2.3, 6.3 and 8.3). The facilitation of FDI operations once established in Ethiopia requires the availability of technical and financial capacity in these institutions. Furthermore, the competence of these institutions has a significant impact on the quantity and quality of FDI in agriculture attracted to Ethiopia. Strengthening the capacity of social and economic sector institutions that are also crucial for the facilitation and scrutiny of sustainable and pro-poor agricultural investments is important. These institutions include education, health, infrastructure, labour, environment and policing (see Sections 6.2.4, 6.2.5, 6.2.6, 6.2.7, 6.2.8 and 6.2.9).

The chosen theoretical framework of this research – critical realism – was appropriate and allowed the research to answer questions relating to pro-poor and environmentally sustainable FDI in Ethiopia. This research investigated issues related to FDI and agricultural land tenure in Ethiopia. It drew the data from different interest groups, namely the government of Ethiopia, investor companies and the communities where these investments occurred. As they all had different perceptions and experiences of the impact of FDI in large-scale agriculture, it was important to be able to hear the various voices and to establish a "collection of answers" for its research questions. Adopting critical realism as its philosophical grounding set the scene for combining research approaches in order to critically assess the complex and sensitive issues of FDI in large-scale agriculture in Ethiopia. The research was value-aware as it was conducted in the social world, which is not a closed system like a laboratory, and informants spoke from their perspectives only. The chosen paradigm supported the use of a case study method that, in turn, facilitated the use of different techniques such as document review, interviews and direct observation to collect and validate data (see Appendices 1, 2 and 3).

The multiple case study methodology applied in this research was appropriate to answer questions on sensitive and contentious issues requiring a systematic method of data collection and processing in order to fully understand the situation (see Chapter 7). It also required an in-depth investigation of the various policies and policy-based proclamation documents (see Section 6.2). The effect of these on the ground was assessed through interviewing key informants, namely government officials at all levels of government, company representatives and community residents, and making direct observations of the cases (see Appendices 1 and 3). The multiple case study method facilitated a cross-case analysis. The case studies enabled triangulation of the information gathered from various informants and of the research findings, thus strengthening internal rigour. FDI in large-scale agriculture in Ethiopia is concentrated in three emerging regions, two of which were included in this research. The third region shares similar contexts with those two, and hence, the results of the study can be generalisable to that region as well (See Figure 7.2).

The research identified and applied two main analytical frameworks to assess the investment policy as well as relevant sectors' policies' contents and implementation in support of pro-poor and environmentally sustainable FDI in large-scale agriculture. These analytical frameworks were derived from various principles and measures to promote environmentally sustainable and pro-poor FDI in large-scale agriculture. It included aspects related to land and resource rights of indigenous people, agricultural workers' rights, food security, transparency and good governance, consultation and participation, social and environmental sustainability and economic viability (see Section 3.7). These frameworks were applied to assess the performance of the agricultural projects and included issues related to social, environmental and economic.

The study concludes that the contents of the Ethiopian investment and sectors' policies and policy-based proclamations are sound and capture each aspect that is significant to promote pro-poor and environmentally sustainable FDI in large-scale agriculture (see Section 6.2). This is in line with the global and regional frameworks and guidelines in national investment strategies, policies, laws, rules and programmes for effective agricultural sector development (see Section 3.9). However, the support provided by the institutions that implement the Investment Policy is minimal as evidenced from the assessment of the cases against the pro-poor and environmentally sustainable investment criteria (see Section 3.8 and Appendix 4). The results point towards the need for the policy to strengthen the capacity of relevant institutions to promote, assess and control FDI in large-scale agriculture and their impacts. The investigation also reveals lack of capacity within the FDI in terms of pro-poor, environmentally sustainable and economically viable large-scale agriculture project delivery.

9.2 Implications

Pro-poor and environmentally sustainable FDI in large-scale agriculture could certainly contribute to agricultural transformation and sustainable rural development. Its realisation requires strong institutions particularly those in the social, economic and environmental sectors. These institutions could ensure the availability of skilled labour that corresponds to the needs of FDI at different stages of its operations, infrastructures and social stability. These are vital elements for success in operations of inward FDI. In addition, the institutions tasked with promoting investment should have the capacity to attract investors who have the experience and capacity to deal with environmentally sustainable, socially beneficial and economically viable large-scale agriculture. Hence, the Ethiopian institutions that are entrusted with facilitating FDI in large-scale agriculture need to strengthen their human and financial capacities, as well as balance the number of FDI projects with their available human resources, in order to manage these projects effectively.[1] Further research on how to mobilise resources to provide the needed infrastructure, avail a skilled workforce and strengthen the capacity of institutions are recommended.

The communities' local knowledge of the ecology is very important to make large-scale agricultural investments environmentally sustainable and socially beneficial. Their involvement in the process of large-scale agricultural investments should be included in LUP. Their role in the negotiation of large-scale land leases is paramount for the success of the agricultural investments. The government needs to facilitate the full engagement of local communities in the planning and implementation processes to ensure pro-poor and environmentally sustainable FDI in large-scale agriculture.

Other suggestions include a further study on the economic and social impacts of flooding in Bildak and Knjikocho Kebeles, both in the Jikao District, and Pino Kebele in Itang Special District of Gambella Regional State, wherein the Karuturi large-scale agricultural project is located (see Section 7.3.1.2).

The eco-tourism industry has also been found to enhance the conservation of the environment, to improve the well-being of the local people and to contribute to the national economic development. Its numerous benefits have been documented in other countries such as Kenya and Cost Rica. It should be investigated as a suitable area of development for Gambella and Beneshangul-Gumuz regions, which are endowed with natural resources (see Section 7.2). The Gambella National Park is a sanctuary for some of the most exquisite wildlife in the world and one of the region's treasures. However, the Park is facing encroachments by large-scale agricultural projects. Further research on how to form, finance and manage the eco-tourism industry and an assessment of the sociocultural, economic and environmental impacts of the eco-tourism investment, including its workability in Ethiopia, is recommended. This may also enable a future comparison between large-scale agricultural investment and eco-tourism investment in terms of their long-term benefits to the environmental, economic and social development, as well as their comparable economic costs and benefits.

Note

1 Minimise the number of FDI to regularly monitor and give adequate support. This allows the quick identification of problems related to the investment and appropriate measures to be made timely.

Appendix 1

Interviewees[1]

Regional Level

Item #	Name of Institutions	Department/Office	
1	Land Utilisation, Administration and Environmental Protection Authority	Environmental Protection Unit	EPU, 2014
		Land Utilisation and Administration unit	LUAU, 2014
2	Agricultural Development Bureau	Sustainable Natural Resources Development, Protection and Utilization Unit	SNRDPUU, 2014
		Forest Resource Administration, Protection & Utilisation Unit	FRAPUU, 2014
		Crop production and Protection Unit	CPAPU, 2014
3	Labour and Social Affairs Bureau	Labour Market & Employment Information Service Unit	LMEISU, 2014
4	Investment Bureau	Investment Bureau General Directorate	IBGD, 2014
5	Statistics Bureau	Statistics Bureau General Directorate	SBGD, 2014
6	Wildlife Conservation Authority	Wildlife Conservation Office	WICO, 2014
7	Horn of Africa Gambella Regional Environment and Network	Environment and Network Office	ENO, 2014

District Level			*Kebele Level (Lowest Unit of Government)*		
Item #	Name of District Administrative Office		Item #	Name of Kebele	
1	Goge District	GODI1, 2014	1	Wathgac Kebele	WATKE, 2014
		GODssI2, 2014	2	Illia Kebele	ILIKE, 2014
2	Abobo District	ABDI, 2014	3	Pukedi Kebele	PUKE, 2014
3	Itang Special District	ITDI, 2014	4	Perbengo Kebele	PERKE, 2014
			5	Uleng/Pugnido Kebele	ULEKE, 2014

Foreign Investor Companies

Item #	Name of Investor Companies	Level of Key Informants	
1	Saudi Star Agricultural Development PLC	Senior Management	SADP-SM, 2014
		Factory workers	SADP-FW, 2014
2	Ruchi Agri PLC	Senior Management	RAP-SM, 2014

Foreign Investor Companies

Item #	Name of Investor Companies	Level of Key Informants	
3	Karuturi Agro Products PLC	Senior Management	KAPP-SM, 2014
4	Toren Agro Industries PLC	Senior Management	TAIP-SM1, 2014
		Senior Management	TAIP-SM2, 2014
5	S&P (Shaporji) Energy Solutions PLC	Senior Management	SESP-SM, 2014
6	BHO Bio Products	Farmworkers	BBP-FW, 2014

Village Level

Item #	Focus Group Discussions		Item #	Individual Interviews with Community Elder	
1	Wathgac Community	WATCO, 2014	1	Wathgac Community	WATCO-EL, 2014
2	Illia Community	ILICO, 2014	2	Illia Community	ILICO-EL, 2014
3	Pukedi Community	PUKCO, 2014	3	Pukedi Community	PUKCO-EL, 2014
4	Perbengo Community	PERCO, 2014	4	Perbengo Community	PERCO-EL, 2014
5	Uleng/Pugnido Community	ULECO, 2014	5	Uleng/Pugnido Community	ULECO-EL, 2014

Note

1 Given the sensitivity of the issue studied, source protection was deemed important, and hence, codes are used instead of the participants' real names.

Appendix 2
Lists of documents used

1 Policies and proclamations

1.1 Imperial regime policies and proclamations

- Personal and Business Tax Proclamation No. 107/1949; Negarit Gazette, Addis Ababa, 1949.
- Investment Proclamation No. 242/1966; Negarit Gazette, Addis Ababa, 1966.
- Proclamation No. 140/1954 to amend the personal and business tax proclamation no. 107/1949, Negarit Gazette, 14th Year No. 1, Addis Ababa, 20th September 1954.
- Development in Ethiopia 1941–1964, Ministry of Information, The Imperial Ethiopian Government, 1941, Addis Ababa, Ethiopia.
- Development in Ethiopia 1941–1964, Ministry of Information, The Imperial Ethiopian Government, 1964, Addis Ababa, Ethiopia.
- Agriculture in Ethiopia, Publications and Foreign Languages Press Department, The Imperial Ethiopian Government, 1964, Addis Ababa, Ethiopia.
- Ethiopia Today: Investment Opportunities, Ministry of Information, The Imperial Ethiopian Government, July 1973, Addis Ababa, Ethiopia.

1.2 Military regime policies and proclamations

- Declaration on Economic Policy of Socialist Ethiopia, (1975), Addis Ababa, February 7, 1975.
- Proclamation No. 26/1975 for the ownership and control by the government of the means of production, Negarit Gazette, 34th year, No. 22, Addis Ababa, 11th March 1975.
- Proclamation No. 31/1975 for the public ownership of rural lands, Negarit Gazette, 9th April 1975, Addis Ababa, The Provisional Military Administration Council.
- Proclamation No. 47 of 1975 for government ownership of urban lands and extra urban houses, Negarit Gazette, 26th July 1975, Addis Ababa, The Provisional Military Administration Council.

- Regulations for the Establishment of Agricultural Development Corporations, Negarit Gazette, No. 21, Addis Ababa, 20th February 1976; Negarit Gazette, No. 27, Addis Ababa, 23rd March 1976.
- Regulations No. 10/1990 for the participation of foreign investors. Negarit Gazette, 49th year, No. 23, Council of Ministers, Addis Ababa, 4th September, 1990.
- Special Decree No. 17/1990 on Investment, Negarit Gazette, 49th year, No. 12, Council of State, Addis Ababa, 19th May, 1990.

1.3 EPRDF regime policies, proclamations and strategies

- Environmental Policy, Environmental Protection Authority, (1997), Federal Democratic Republic of Ethiopia, Addis Ababa.
- Ethiopia's Climate Resilient Green Economy Strategy, Environmental Protection Authority, (2011), Federal Democratic Republic of Ethiopia, Addis Ababa.
- Education and Training Policy, Ministry of Education, (1994), Federal Democratic Republic Government of Ethiopia, Addis Ababa, April 1994.
- National Adult Education Strategy, Ministry of Education, (2008), Federal Democratic Republic Government of Ethiopia, Addis Ababa, February 2008.
- Health Policy and Strategies, Ministry of Health, (1993), Transitional Government of Ethiopia, Addis Ababa, September 1993.
- Rural Development Policy and Strategies, Ministry of Finance and Economic Development, Economic Policy and Planning Department, (2003), Government of the Federal Democratic Republic of Ethiopia, Addis Ababa, April 2003.
- Growth and Transformation Plan, Ministry of Finance and Economic Development, (2010), Government of the Federal Democratic Republic of Ethiopia, Addis Ababa, September 2010.
- National Social Protection Policy of Ethiopia, Final draft, Ministry of Labour and Social Affairs, 26 March 2012.
- Environmental Impact Assessment Proclamation No. 299/2002, Federal Negarit Gazette, 9th Year, No. 11, Addis Ababa, 3 December 2002.
- Environmental Pollution Control Proclamation No. 300/2002, Federal Negarit Gazette, 9th Year, No. 12, Addis Ababa, 3 December 2002.
- Expropriation of Landholdings for Public Purposes and Payment of Compensation Proclamation No. 455/2005, Federal NegaritGazeta, 11th Year No. 43, 15 July 2005.
- Investment Proclamation No. 769/2012, Federal Negarit Gazette, 18th Year, No.63, Addis Ababa, 17 September 2012.
- Labour Proclamation No. 377/2003, Federal Negarit Gazette, 10th Year, No. 12, Addis Ababa, 26 February 2004.
- Labour Proclamations No.466/2005, Federal Negarit Gazette, 11th Year, No. 56, Addis Ababa, 30 June 2005.
- Labour Proclamation No. 494/2006, Federal Negarit Gazette, 12th Year, No. 30, Addis Ababa, 29 June 2006.

- Proclamation No. 269/2012 for the establishment of the Ethiopian Investment Agency, Federal Negarit Gazette, 19th Year, No. 2, Addis Ababa, 23 November 2012.
- Proclamation No.803/2013 for the establishment of the Ministry of Environment and Forest, Federal Negarit Gazette, 19th Year, No. 61, Addis Ababa, 29 July 2013.
- Proclamation No. 313/2014 for the establishment of the Ethiopian Investment Commission, Federal Negarit Gazette, 20th Year, No. 63, Addis Ababa, 14 August 2014.
- Proclamation No. 283/2013 for the establishment of the Ethiopian Agricultural Investment Land Administration Agency, Federal Negarit Gazette, 19th Year, No. 32, Addis Ababa, 4 March 2013.
- Proclamation No.7/1992 for the establishment of National/Regional Self-government, NegaritGazeta, 51st Year, No. 2, 1992a, Transitional Government of Ethiopia, Addis Ababa.
- Proclamation of the Constitution of the Federal Democratic Republic of Ethiopia No.1/1995 – Federal Nagarit Gazette, 1st Year, No. 1, Addis Ababa, 21 August 1995.
- Rural Land Administration and Use Proclamation No. 456/2005, Federal Negarit Gazette, 11th Year, No.44, Addis Ababa, 15 July 2005.
- Solid Waste Management Proclamation No. 513/2007, Federal Negarit Gazette, 13th Year No. 13, Addis Ababa, 12 February 2007.

2 Guidelines and codes of practice

- Guideline to prepare project documents on environmental impact assessment for agricultural investments, Ministry of Agriculture, April 2010.
- Environmental Code of Practice for Agricultural investment, Ministry of Agriculture, June 2010.
- An Investment Guide to Ethiopia: Opportunities and Conditions, Ethiopian Investment Agency, 2013.
- Factor Cost (i.e. land, labour, etc.), Ethiopian Investment Agency, June 2013.

3 Gambella regional state's rules and regulations

- Rural land administration and land use.
- Agricultural investment.
- Labour.
- Environmental protection.

4 Beneshangul-Gumuz regional state's rules and regulations

- Rural land administration and land use.
- Agricultural investments.

- Labour.
- Environmental protection.

5 Investment contractual agreements of this research case studies

- Saudi Star Agricultural Development PLC.
- Karuturi Agro Products PLC.
- BHO Bio Products PLC.
- Ruchi Agri PLC.
- Toren Agro Products PLC.
- Shamporji Energy Solutions PLC.

6 Environmental impact assessment reports

- Saudi Star Agricultural Development PLC.
- Toren Agro Industries PLC.
- Karuturi Agro Products PLC.
- BHO Bio Products PLC.

7 Reports on FDI in agricultural land in Ethiopia

- The 2009 FAO's Report on Agricultural Investment and Proposed Land Lease Charges in Ethiopia.
- The 2011 FAO's Mid-term Review Report on Technical Assistance for Capacity Building of the Agricultural Investment Support Directorate of Ethiopia which is now upgraded to a full-fledged agency and called Ethiopian Agricultural Investment Land Administration Agency (EAILAA).

Appendix 3
Checklist for direct observation of agricultural projects' sites

Materials to be reviewed:

- Maps and charts of the geographical characteristics or layouts of the study areas (Mapping Agency)
- Population survey data (demographic data) from 2000 of the study areas (Statistics Agency)

Other items to observe at the site:

The compliance for proper agriculture investment land utilisation of this code of conduct is the following:

- Windbreak indigenous trees are cultivated/the trees along the river banks are not cut down,
- The land area in the distance of 1.5–2 kilometres is left untouched,
- Agronomic practices implemented are not exposing the land to soil erosion, and
- Indigenous trees are planted on 5% of the leased land.

The compliance for maintaining and improving social and cultural aspects of the farming place and the surrounding is the following:

- Historical relics, burial sites and cultural monuments are fenced and left untouched while ploughing;
- Involve the local people in the whole process of planning and implementation of the project; and
- Settlement areas of farmworkers, families and surrounding community should be at least 2 kilometres away from farm area.

Region	Farm Location	Type of Production	Size and Date of Land Leased	Investor company's name and Nationalities	Observed Items							
					Geographical Characteristics/ Layouts of the study area	Windbreak indigenous trees are cultivated	The land area in the distance of 1.5–2km is left untouched	Proportion of developed leased land (in December 2014)	Agronomic Practices implemented are not exposing the land to soil erosion while ploughing	Historical relics, burial sites and cultural monuments are fenced and left untouched while ploughing	Involve the local people in the whole process of planning and implementation of the project	Settlement areas of farmworkers, families and surrounding community should be at least 2kms away from the farm area
Gambella	Agnuwak Zone, Abobo District, between Perbengo and Pukedi Kebele	Rice	10,000 ha on 29 September 2009 (50 year lease)	Saudi Star Agricultural Development PLC. Saudi Arabian	Dense forestlands, rivers	No	No	They are supposed to develop all the hectares leased by the 4th year, but are now in the 5th and have developed just 3.5% of the land (350 ha of 10,000 ha).	Trees are cleared, and rice is the main production. Excessive water usage, and there is no water recycling method. Use of fertilisers and waste damping	No	Not at all	The farm is located between forest and rivers, and the closest town is at least 10 km away. The workers' camp is more than 2 km away.
	Itang Special District, Wanke Kebele	Cereal crops, pulses and edible oil crops	27,000 ha on 11 May 2010 (25 years lease)	BHO Bio products PLC. Indian	Savanna grassland, river	No	No information as the author denied visiting the farm.	No information as the author denied visiting the farm site and conducting interviews. However, according to the contract they are supposed to develop 100% of the land at the 4th year after signing.	Maize is the main production. The biggest concern is chemical use, storage and damping waste. Also excessive water usage and no recycling method.	No	Not at all	The community lives about 5kms away, and opposite the farm. The workers' camp is 2 km away.

(Continued)

(Continued)

Region	Farm Location	Type of Production	Size and Date of Land Leased	Investor company's name and Nationalities	Observed Items							
					Geographical Characteristics/ Layouts of the study area	Windbreak trees are cultivated	The land area in the distance of 1.5–2km is left untouched	Proportion of developed leased land (in December 2014)	Agronomic Practices implemented are not exposing the land to soil erosion	Historical relics, burial sites and cultural monuments are fenced and left untouched while ploughing	Involve the local people in the whole process of planning and implementation of the project	Settlement areas of farmworkers, families and surrounding community should be at least 2kms away from the farm area
	Nuer Zone, Jikao District and Itang Special District	Palm cereals, rice and sugarcane	100,000 ha on October 25 2010, but the initial agreement was done with the district on 4 August 2008 (50 years lease)	Karuturi Agro products PLC. Indian	Dense Forestlands, rivers	No	No	The company is supposed to develop 100% of the land in 2 years from signing the contract. It is now 6 years later, and they have only developed 30% of the land (30,000 ha of 100,000 ha).	Maize, soya bean and sesame are the main plantation. The maize that was planted in the 30,000 ha of land has vanished due to floods which were caused mainly by its construction to block the natural water flow which exacerbated the floods that occur from time to time during the rainy season. These have wiped out the nearby villages and damaged the road in late summer and early fall of 2014. Chemical use, storage and waste damping.	No	Not at all	The company's land stretched to two districts and four kebeles (villages). In Jikaow District, the three villages are not functional due to the flood. It is now operating in one village in Itang Special District (Illia Village); the farm distance is more than 2 km, opposite the village. The workers' camp is also away from the farm, adjacent to the village.

| Agnuwa Zone, Goge District, Puchal, Pugnido and Teta Kebeles | Soybeans | 25,000 ha on 5 April 2010, (25 years lease) | Ruchi Agri PLC, Indian | Forestlands including shea butter trees | No | There are some trees, but it is difficult to measure the distance. | The company is supposed to have developed 100% of the land in 4 years from contract signing, but only 14% has been developed by this point (3,500 ha out of the 25,000 ha). | Maize, soya bean and groundnuts are the main crops. Chemical applied, stored and waste damping. Water is used in excess with no recycling method. | No | Not at all | The villagers are away from the farms. The workers' camp is more than 2 km away and in opposite the farm. |

Remark: All the visited farms leased forestlands, woodlands or savanna lands, and no village is evicted in order to provide the land to investors.

Appendix 4

Qualitative assessment of the case study FDIs

... on pro-poor investment

Performance assessment rating system: 1 = poor, 2 = fair, 3 = average, 4 = good, 5 = very good.

Pro-poor investment criteria	Case studies agricultural projects					
	Karuturi	Saudi Star	Ruchi	Toren	BHO	S&P[1]
Existing rights to natural resources are recognised and respected	1	1	1	1	1	1
Participation of local residents, especially indigenous people, in the negotiation of large-scale land lease	1	1	1	1	1	1
Improvement of local farmers' farming methods	1	1	1	1	1	1
Improvement of local population's food security	1	1	1	1	1	1
Creation of jobs for local population	3	2	1	4	1	NA
Agricultural products (i.e. staple[2] vs non-staple; food crops vs industrial crops)[3]	2	1	2	3	2	1
Respecting the core labour standards including wages, working hours, health insurance, occupational health and safety and other benefits	2	2	1	5	1	NA
Labour-intensive technology is used to create more jobs for the locals	1	1	1	1	1	1
Out-grower scheme is practised (i.e. creation of direct linkage between the project and local smallholder farmers)	1	1	1	1	1	1
Support to improve the local community's road, schools and health centres (i.e. Corporate Social Responsibility)	3	1	1	4	1	NA
Total Score = 50	**16**	**12**	**11**	**22**	**11**	**7**
Environmental impacts of the project are quantified	2	2	1	2	2	1
Measures taken to mitigate the negative impacts of the project	1	2	1	3	1	1
Measures taken to ensure sustainable use of resources	1	1	1	1	1	1
Agricultural wastes are managed as per industry best practice	1	1	1	4	1	NA
Agrochemicals are managed as per Environmental Code of Practice for Agricultural investment	1	1	1	4	1	NA
Total Score = 25	**6**	**7**	**5**	**14**	**6**	**3**
Grand Total Score: 50 + 25 = 75	**22**	**19**	**16**	**36**	**17**	**10**

[1] S&P – The study was not able to make a direct observation on the farm site and its surroundings. Hence, three of the pro-poor criteria cannot be assessed (i.e. 15 points), and two of the environmentally sustainable criteria (i.e. 10 points) cannot be assessed.

[2] Case study areas' staple foods are maize, sorghum and millet.

[3] Industrial crops are crops that provide material inputs for industrial processes and products such as oil crops, textile crops and biofuel crops. Its production potentially competes with food crops for land, water and other factors of production. The end product might not be available for the local population.

Karuturi's total score on pro-poor and environmentally sustainable investment

Pro-poor criteria	Karuturi's performance	Results	Score
Existing rights to natural resources are recognised and respected	The communities' forest and savanna grassland are leased by the project. The communities are denied access to the natural resources which was their livelihoods. The project also leased the communities' ancestors/lords cemetery places. The communities didn't get any compensation for losing their livelihoods	Poor	1
Participation of local residents, especially indigenous people, in the negotiation of large-scale land lease	The communities were not consulted about the project beforehand. They came to know when the project started cutting trees, savanna grasses and building its camp	Poor	1
Improvement of local farmers' farming methods	The project is highly mechanised and uses high tech while the communities using primitive tools. No support has been given in upgrading their farming methods and increase production	Poor	1
Improvements of local population's food security	The project's principal products are palm, cereals and pulses for export. It doesn't contribute directly to the local population food security. In fact, the project leases the forestland where the community used to collect stem plants to supplement their food needs during dry season. It also leases the savanna grassland where their animals graze. The community doesn't now have access to these resources.	Poor	1
Creation of jobs for local population	Labourer and machine operation jobs. It also gave training for local people who are engaged in operating machines such as tractors. Ethiopians from other part of the country are hired as mechanics and drivers	Average	3
Agricultural products (i.e. staple[4] vs non-staple; food crops vs industrial crops)[5]	The project principal products are non-staple. It produced maize for trial purposes which is the local population staple food.	Fair	2
Respecting the core labour standards including wages, working hours, health insurance, occupational health and safety and other benefits	The project pays the labourers ETB 25/day which is less than the standard rate ETB 50/day. No health insurance while on duty. Occupational health and safety measures are not taken. The projects provide food for workers	Fair	2
Labour-intensive technology is used to create more jobs for the locals	It is highly mechanised and thus it creates a few jobs compared to its investment size. The labourer jobs are seasonal.	Poor	1
Out-grower scheme is practised (i.e. creation of direct linkage between the project and local smallholder farmers)	Direct linkage is not practised. The agricultural lease agreement doesn't encourage creating linkages with local smallholder farmers. This could also pave ways to upgrade their farming method and increase productivity.	Poor	1
Support to improve the local community's road, schools and health centres (i.e. Corporate Social	The project shares electric power, generated by diesel generator, with the nearby clinic to give service in the evening. The project avails transport to the community during health emergency. When the project car is going to town, it gives rides to the community as there is no public transport.	Average	3

Environmental sustainability criteria	Karuturi's performance	Results	Scores
Environmental impacts of the project are quantified	The project's Environmental and Social Impact Assessment (E&SIA) was conducted after three years of commencing its operation where its significant adverse impacts are quantified and mitigation measures are spelled out. This is in breach of the EIA Proclamation No. 299/2002 which state the EIA of projects should be undertaken before commencing the project.	Fair	2
Measures taken to mitigate the negative impacts of the project	The mitigation measures are not taken. For instance, one of the measures is the project to establish an Environmental and Social Affairs Unit in order to implement the rest of the mitigation measures identified in the E&SIA report of the project. The E&SIA study report affirmed that the Karuturi agricultural project can only be feasible if the project implements the SIMP of the study without delay.	Poor	1
Measures taken to ensure sustainable use of resources	The project leases forest and savanna lands which it started clearing. Some of these lands belong to the national park. The project doesn't follow the lease agreement which states the project to plant indigenous trees on 5% of the leased land and to leave windbreak indigenous trees. The project doesn't have a water management system such as water recycling plant to save this non-renewable resources for future generation, although water is now in abundant in the area. It doesn't have a plan to offset its carbon footprints and promote sustainable agricultural practices.	Poor	1
Agricultural waste are managed as per industry best practice	The project doesn't have waste management system. Agricultural waste are damped into the environment.	Poor	1
Agrochemicals are managed as per Environmental Code of Practice for Agricultural investment	The farm doesn't have appropriate place to store agrochemicals. They are stored in metal container.	Poor	1
Total Score = 25			**6**
Grand total score (50 + 25) = 75			**(16 + 6) = 22**

[4] Case study areas' staple foods are maize, sorghum and millet.

[5] Industrial crops are crops that provide material inputs for industrial processes and products such as oil crops, textile crops and biofuel crops. Its production potentially competes with food crops for land, water and other factors of production. The end product might not be available for local the population.

Saudi Star's total score on pro-poor and environmentally sustainable investment

Pro-poor criteria	Saudi Star's performance	Results	Score
Existing rights to natural resources are recognised and respected	The project land was covered by dense forest which was the communities livelihoods	Poor	1
Participation of local residents, especially indigenous people, in the negotiation of large-scale land lease	The communities was not involved in the negotiation of the agricultural land lease. They came to know when the project started clearing the forestland. The negotiation took place between the government at higher authorities and the investor.	Poor	1
Improvement of local farmers' farming methods	The project is highly mechanised and uses high tech while the communities using primitive tools. No support has been given in upgrading their farming methods and increase production	Poor	1
Improvements of local population's food security	The project principal agricultural product is rice for export. The communities used to collect potato like plant, locally called "Modo/Babure" which helps them to supplement their family food during the time when they have lower crop production.	Poor	1
Creation of jobs for local population	It created seasonal (labourer) jobs for locals. Machine operators and others working in the rice husking factory are from other parts of Ethiopia.	Fair	2
Agricultural products (i.e. staple[6] vs non-staple; food crops vs industrial crops)[7]	The project produces rice, which is not the locals' staple food, for export. The local population's staple foods are sorghum and maize.	Poor	1
Respecting the core labour standards including wages, working hours, health insurance, occupational health and safety and other benefits	The project's labour wage rate is lower than the industry wage standard. The workers don't have proper safety gear which are industry standard to protect them from occupational hazardous.	Fair	2
Labour-intensive technology is used to create more jobs for the locals	The project is highly mechanised. For its size of operation, the project could create more jobs for the locals if it promotes labour-intensive technology.	Poor	1
Out-grower scheme is practised (i.e. creation of direct linkage between the project and local smallholder farmers)	There is no linkages between the project and local smallholder farmers. The land-lease contract doesn't encourage out-grower scheme.	Poor	1
Support to improve the local community's road, schools and health centres (i.e. Corporate Social Responsibility)	The project hasn't provided support to improve the local infrastructure, schools and health centre.	Poor	1
			12

Environmental sustainability criteria	Saudi Star's performance	Results	Scores
Environmental impacts of the project are quantified	The project's Environmental and Social Impact Assessment (E&SIA) was conducted after two years of commencing its operation where its significant adverse impacts are quantified and mitigation measures are spelled out. This is in breach of the EIA Proclamation No. 299/2002 which states the EIA of projects should be undertaken before commencing the project	Fair	2
Measures taken to mitigate the negative impacts of the project	The mitigation measures are not adequately implemented. The project doesn't have an EMU or expert to advise and monitor the environmental performance of the farm, including the adequate implementation of the mitigation measures for the adverse impact of the farm activities.	Fair	2
Measures taken to ensure sustainable use of resources	The project leases forestlands surrounded with wetlands and rivers. Wetlands are sensitive, and agricultural practice adversely affects the wetlands. The project cleared the forest which is the natural habitat for a number of species of flora and fauna. Rice is the main production, and it requires the usage of excessive water. The project doesn't have a water management system to ensure sustainable use of water. The project doesn't follow the lease agreement which states the project to plant indigenous trees on 5% of the leased land and to leave windbreak indigenous trees. It doesn't have a plan to offset its carbon footprints and promote sustainable agricultural practices.	Poor	1
Agricultural waste are managed as per industry best practice	The project doesn't have waste management system. Agricultural waste are damped into the environment. It doesn't have a designated landfilled for solid waste. It burns the solid waste.	Poor	1
Agrochemicals are managed as per Environmental Code of Practice for Agricultural investment	The farm doesn't have appropriate place to store agrochemicals such as fertilisers and pesticides. They are stored in metal container. In addition, the different chemicals are stored together without categorising it by name and composition of active ingredients.	Poor	1
Total Score = 25			**7**
Grand total score (50 + 25) = 75			**(12 + 7) = 19**

[6] Case study areas' staple foods are maize, sorghum and millet.
[7] Industrial crops are crops that provide material inputs for industrial processes and products such as oil crops, textile crops and biofuel crops. Its production potentially competes with food crops for land, water and other factors of production. The end product might not be available for the local population.

Ruchi's total score on pro-poor and environmentally sustainable investment

Pro-poor criteria	Ruchi's performance	Results	Score
Existing rights to natural resources are recognised and respected	The project land was forestland which was covered mainly by Shea trees which was the communities' livelihoods.	Poor	1
Participation of local residents, especially indigenous people, in the negotiation of large-scale land lease	The communities was not involved in the negotiation of the agricultural land lease. They came to know when the project started deploying the farm machineries and cutting the trees.	Poor	1
Improvement of local farmers' farming methods	The project is highly mechanised and uses high tech while the communities using primitive tools. No support has been given in upgrading their farming methods and increase production.	Poor	1
Improvements of local population's food security	The project principal agricultural product is oil crops such as soybeans, groundnuts, sorghum, rice and maize for export. The communities used to collect Shea fruits which were their livelihood. They now don't have access to the forest resources, and most of the trees which were in their proximity are gone.	Poor	1
Creation of jobs for local population	It created seasonal (labourer) jobs for locals who quite due to long working hours without overtime payment.	Poor	1
Agricultural products (i.e. staple[8] vs non-staple; food crops vs industrial crops)[9]	The project produces sorghum and maize which is the locals' staple food, though it produces these crops to make oil for export. It doesn't yet have an oil refinery in Ethiopia.	Fair	2
Respecting the core labour standards including wages, working hours, health insurance, occupational health and safety and other benefits	The project doesn't provide adequate accommodation for the labourers who are from other parts of Ethiopia and they cannot commute every day like the workers from the community. Long working hours without overtime payment. The project doesn't have a contractual agreement when employing the farmworkers which is against the Ethiopian Labour Proclamation No 377/2003, Article 4, Sub Articles 3 & 5.	Poor	1
Labour-intensive technology is used to create more jobs for the locals	The project is highly mechanised. For its size of the operation, the project could create more jobs for the locals if it promotes labour-intensive technology.	Poor	1
Out-grower scheme is practised (i.e. creation of direct linkage between the project and local smallholder farmers)	There is no linkages between the project and local smallholder farmers. The land lease contract doesn't encourage out-grower scheme.	Poor	1
Support to improve the local community's road, schools and health centres (i.e. Corporate Social Responsibility)	The project hasn't provided support to improve the local infrastructures, schools and health centre.	Poor	1
Total Score = 50			**11**

Environmental sustainability criteria	Ruchi's performance	Results	Scores
Environmental impacts of the project are quantified	The project's EIA report was not found neither at the farm site nor at the EAILAA, which is the sole responsible agency to handle agricultural-related environmental and social impact assessment issues. The EIA report should be a working manual and available at the farm. This shows that the report was prepared just to comply with the rules rather than to make a real impact on the ground. For instance, the farm is in proximity with Gambella National Park which harbours quite a number of wild animals. The location of the farm denies the animals' access to seasonal pastures or water points. These adverse impacts of the project could be captured and quantified, and mitigation measures should have been taken.	Poor	1
Measures taken to mitigate the negative impacts of the project	The project doesn't have the EIA report at the site. It doesn't have an EMU or expert to advise and monitor the environmental performance of the farm including ensuring the adequate implementation of the mitigation measures for the adverse impact of the farm activities.	Poor	1
Measures taken to ensure sustainable use of resources	The project cleared the trees without giving due consideration to the signed contractual agreement which clearly specifies the number of indigenous trees to be left per hectare of land. The project doesn't have a water management system to ensure sustainable use of water. It doesn't have a plan to offset its carbon footprints and promote sustainable agricultural practices. This shows the project lack of consideration into the environment and sustainable farming.	Poor	1
Agricultural waste are managed as per industry best practice	The project doesn't have waste management system. Agricultural waste are damped into the environment. Empty chemical containers are buried in the ground. There is a high risk of soil and groundwater contamination.	Poor	1
Agrochemicals are managed as per Environmental Code of Practice for Agricultural investment	The farm doesn't have appropriate place to store agrochemicals. It has a small room where hand tools, spraying instruments, construction materials and agrochemicals are stored together. This doesn't comply with the Environmental Code of Practice for Agricultural Investment. This code of practice is a minimum standard and a mandatory to all large-scale farms.	Poor	1

Total Score = 25
Grand total score (50 + 25) = 75 (11 + 5) = 17   5

---

8 Case study areas' staple foods are maize, sorghum and millet.

9 Industrial crops are crops that provide material inputs for industrial processes and products such as oil crops, textile crops and biofuel crops. Its production potentially competes with food crops for land, water and other factors of production. The end product might not be available for the local population.

Toren's total score on pro-poor and environmentally sustainable investment

Pro-poor criteria	Toren's performance	Results	Score
Existing rights to natural resources are recognised and respected	The project land was woodland and surrounded by river. These resources were the communities' livelihoods. The woodlands were used to hang the beehives which the communities produce and sell honey. Fishing is one of the resources of food and income for the communities. The project extensively irrigates from the river which could affect fish production.	Poor	1
Participation of local residents, especially indigenous people, in the negotiation of large-scale land lease	The communities were not involved in the negotiation of the agricultural land lease.	Poor	1
Improvement of local farmers' farming methods	The project is highly mechanised and uses high tech while the communities using primitive tools.	Poor	1
Improvements of local population's food security	The project principal agricultural product is cotton, with soybeans as a rotational crop. The clearing of the woodlands affects the wild animals which the communities used to hunt during shortage of food. The widely hunted animal is the antelope which was used a coping mechanism for securing food for the family.	Poor	1
Creation of jobs for local population	The project gives job priority to nearby villagers, then residents of Gog District and Gambella Region with the view of giving job opportunities for the communities. If they don't find in Gambella, they then hire from other parts of Ethiopia. They also give training for Ethiopian employees in operating and maintaining the various high-tech machines such as tractors and GPS-guided levelling equipment.	Good	4
Agricultural products (i.e. staple[10] vs non-staple; food crops vs industrial crops)[11]	The project's principal product is cotton which is a non-staple and industrial crop. For a tryout, the project produced maize to be used for employees' food as most of them are from the surrounding communities whose staple food is maize. The surplus will be sold at the local market.	Average	3
Respecting the core labour standards including wages, working hours, health insurance, occupational health and safety and other benefits	The project's salary rates are very attractive and above the Ethiopian wage standard for the industry. It pays a daily labourer in range ETB 55 to 60 whereas the standard wage rate is ETB 50. It pays a pension, medical expenses, and a hardship allowance to its fixed-term employees. It provides fully equipped housing, food and certified water for drinking. The project provides training and adequate safety gear for workers who handle chemicals. Special medication is available at the farm clinic in case of exposure.	Very good	5

		Results	Scores
Labour-intensive technology is used to create more jobs for the locals	The project is highly mechanised. For its size of the operation, the project could create more jobs for the locals if it promotes labour-intensive technology.	Poor	1
Out-grower scheme is practised (i.e. creation of direct linkage between the project and local smallholder farmers)	There is no linkages between the project and local smallholder farmers. The land-lease contract doesn't encourage out-grower scheme.	Poor	1
Support to improve the local community's road, schools and health centres (i.e. Corporate Social Responsibility)	The project has provided support to rehabilitate a 35 km road from the farm site to the district town. It also provided support to the 19 km road construction from the Gog District to Abobo District. It provided support for the maintenance of two schools in the district.	Good	4
Total Score = 35			**22**

Environmental sustainability criteria	Toren's performance	Results	Scores
Environmental impacts of the project are quantified	The project's E&SIA was conducted after two years of commencing its operation where its significant adverse impacts are quantified and mitigation measures are spelled out. It is in breach of the EIA Proclamation No. 299/2002.	Fair	2
Measures taken to mitigate the negative impacts of the project	The project doesn't have an EMU or expert to advise and monitor the farm's environmental performance including the implementation of the action plan for the environmental risk mitigation measures. However, it has established an 11-ha buffer zone and built the workers residences 2 km away from the farm according to the signed lease agreement.	Average	3
Measures taken to ensure sustainable use of resources	The project cleared the woodlands. The project irrigates its cultivation from the river, and it doesn't have a water management system to ensure sustainable use of water. It doesn't have a plan to offset its carbon footprints and promote sustainable agricultural practices.	Poor	1
Agricultural waste are managed as per industry best practice	Agricultural waste is disposed separately in designated area which is made of concrete.	Good	4
Agrochemicals are managed as per Environmental Code of Practice for Agricultural investment	The agrochemicals are stored properly and comply with the Environmental Code of Practice for Agricultural Investment. To this effect, the project received a certificate for good performance and got a permit to bring chemicals	Good	4
Total Score = 25			**14**
Grand total score (50 + 25) = 75			**(22 + 14) = 36**

[10] Case study areas' staple foods are maize, sorghum and millet.

[11] Industrial crops are crops that provide material inputs for industrial processes and products such as oil crops, textile crops and biofuel crops. Its production potentially competes with food crops for land, water and other factors of production. The end product might not be available for the local population.

BHO's total score on pro-poor and environmentally sustainable investment

Pro-poor criteria	BHO's performance	Results	Score
Existing rights to natural resources are recognised and respected	The project land was savanna grassland and surrounded by river. These resources were the communities' livelihoods. They are semi-pastoralist and thus the savanna grassland is used as their animals' grazing land. The project's irrigation canal and storage ponds hinder the community's cattle passing to the grasslands.	Poor	1
Participation of local residents, especially indigenous people, in the negotiation of large-scale land lease	The community was informed about the investment project by the district and regional offices. The negotiation took place between the federal government and the investor. Neither the community nor the district and regional offices were not part of the negotiation.	Poor	1
Improvement of local farmers' farming methods	The project is highly mechanised and uses high tech while the communities using primitive tools.	Poor	1
Improvements of local population's food security	The project principal agricultural product is oil crops for export.	Poor	1
Creation of jobs for local population	Very limited number of labourer work. No job priority for project area residents.	Poor	1
Agricultural products (i.e. staple[12] vs non-staple; food crops vs industrial crops)[13]	The project's principal product is oil crops which are non-staple and industrial crops. It produced maize and did not sell it in the local market. It was sent to the capital, Addis Ababa.	Fair	2
Respecting the core labour standards including wages, working hours, health insurance, occupational health and safety and other benefits	The project pays in range between ETB 31 to 35 per day which is lower than the standard daily fee of ETB 50. The labourers work all calendar days, and there is no overtime payment for weekends and holidays. There is no medical insurance for the labourers during on duty "Occupational Injuries". There is no protection gear given to the workers who handle agrochemicals. This is in breach of the Labour Proclamation No. 377/2003, Articles 12 and 92.	Poor	1
Labour-intensive technology is used to create more jobs for the locals	The project is highly mechanised. For its size of operation, the project could create more jobs for the locals if it promotes labour-intensive technology.	Poor	1
Out-grower scheme is practised (i.e. creation of direct linkage between the project and local smallholder farmers)	There is no linkages between the project and local smallholder farmers. The land-lease contract doesn't encourage out-grower scheme.	Poor	1
Support to improve the local community's road, schools and health centres (i.e. Corporate Social Responsibility)	No support has been given. In fact the project uses the community's water pump which the government installed. Due to excessive use by the project, the pump is broken.	Poor	1
Total Score = 50			**11**

Environmental sustainability criteria	BHO's performance	Results	Scores
Environmental impacts of the project are quantified	The project's E&SIA was conducted after one years commencing its operation where its significant adverse impacts are quantified and mitigation measures are spelled out. It is in breach of the EIA Proclamation No. 299/2002, which states the EIA of projects should be conducted before the commencement of the operation.	Fair	2
Measures taken to mitigate the negative impacts of the project	The project doesn't have an EMU or expert to advise and monitor the farm's environmental performance including the implementation of the action plan for the environmental risk mitigation measures. One of the mitigation measures is to compensate for the clearance of woodlands by panting at least 4 million seedlings. This was not done.	Poor	1
Measures taken to ensure sustainable use of resources	The project cleared the woodlands. The project cultivates its irrigation from the river, and it doesn't have a water management system to ensure sustainable use of water. It doesn't have a plan to offset its carbon footprints and promote sustainable agricultural practices.	Poor	1
Agricultural waste are managed as per industry best practice	The project doesn't have a waste management system. Agricultural waste are disposed into the environment.	Poor	1
Agrochemicals are managed as per Environmental Code of Practice for Agricultural investment	The project doesn't have a proper storage to store agrochemicals as per the Environmental Code of Practice for Agricultural Investment (MoA, 2010), Special Decree on Pesticides (1990) and Pollution Control Proclamation (2002).	Poor	1
Total Score = 25			**6**
Grand total score (50 + 25) = 75			**(11 + 6) = 17**

[12] Case study areas' staple foods are maize, sorghum and millet.
[13] Industrial crops are crops that provide material inputs for industrial processes and products such as oil crops, textile crops and biofuel crops. Its production potentially competes with food crops for land, water and other factors of production. The end product might not be available for the local population.

S&P's total score on pro-poor and environmentally sustainable investment

Pro-poor criteria	S&P's performance	Results	Score
Existing rights to natural resources are recognised and respected	The project land was forestland. These resources were the communities' livelihoods. It is the community's sacred place. The loss of the existing rights to natural resources affects the communities.	Poor	1
Participation of local residents, especially indigenous people, in the negotiation of large-scale land lease	There was no negotiation with the communities. The regional state was not involved in the land deal. The negotiation took place between the federal government and the investor.	Poor	1
Improvement of local farmers' farming methods	The project is highly mechanised and uses high tech while the communities using primitive tools.	Poor	1
Improvements of local population's food security	The project principal agricultural product is biofuel trees for export. The forest was the communities' source of income and food. It was used for livestock rearing, crop production, honey production, bamboo tree harvesting, firewood and wild plants collecting, hunting wild animals, medicinal plants and cassava. In addition, these communities are suffering from food security and malnutrition.	Poor	1
Creation of jobs for local population	Not applicable as this research was not given access to visit the farm site.	–	–
Agricultural products (i.e. staple[14] vs non-staple; food crops vs industrial crops)[15]	The project's principal product is biofuel trees which are non-staple and industrial crops.	Poor	1
Respecting the core labour standards including wages, working hours, health insurance, occupational health and safety and other benefits	Not applicable as this research was not given access to visit the farm site.	–	–
Labour-intensive technology is used to create more jobs for the locals	The project is highly mechanised. For its size of operation, the project could create more jobs for the locals if it promotes labour-intensive technology.	Poor	1
Out-grower scheme is practised (i.e. creation of direct linkage between the project and local smallholder farmers)	There is no linkages between the project and local smallholder farmers. The land lease contract doesn't encourage out-grower scheme.	Poor	1
Support to improve the local community's road, schools and health centres (i.e. Corporate Social Responsibility)	Not applicable as this research was not given access to visit the farm site.	–	–
Total Score = 50			**7**

Environmental sustainability criteria	S&P's performance	Results	Scores
Environmental impacts of the project are quantified	The project's E&SIA report was not found at the EAILAA or Ministry of Environment and Forest or at the project. There is no information if the adverse impacts of the project are captured and quantified or not.	Poor	1
Measures taken to mitigate the negative impacts of the project	It is difficult to take measures to mitigate the adverse impacts of the project without the EIA report of the project.	Poor	1
Measures taken to ensure sustainable use of resources	The project cleared the forestlands. The cut trees are left to decay at the farm. The project irrigates its cultivation from the river, and it doesn't have a water management system to ensure sustainable use of water. It doesn't have a plan to offset its carbon footprints and promote sustainable agricultural practices.	Poor	1
Agricultural waste is managed as per industry best practice	Not applicable as this research was not given access to visit the farm site.	–	–
Agrochemicals are managed as per Environmental Code of Practice for Agricultural investment	Not applicable as this research was not given access to visit the farm site.	–	–
Total Score = 15			**3**
Grand total score (35 + 15) = 50		**(7 + 3) = 10**	

[14] Case study areas' staple foods are maize, sorghum and millet.

[15] Industrial crops are crops that provide material inputs for industrial processes and products such as oil crops, textile crops and biofuel crops. Its production potentially competes with food crops for land, water and other factors of production. The end product might not be available for the local population.

Glossary

The research uses commonly used terms such as *pro-poor*, *sustainability* and *FDI*. These terms, especially *sustainability*, can be unclear at times because of the various synonyms used in various fields. It is, therefore, important to explain the meaning of these terms in this research.

Command Economy: an economic system whereby the means of production such as land, labour and capital are state-owned and the economic activity is highly controlled by the central authority.

Economic Infrastructure: a subset of the infrastructure sector and includes electric power, transport and communication.

Environmentally Sustainable FDI in Large-Scale Agriculture: FDI in large-scale agriculture but, in addition, the investment is designed to yield long-term benefits as well as being mindful of the environmental effects of development. The FDI should improve the local or regional economy in the host country, it should bind to the rule of law (such as labour law, environmental law) and exercise industry best practices. Such best practices may include farming methods, respecting the local agro-ecological conditions and not accelerating climate change, soil depletion and the exhaustion of freshwater reserves. Training for local farmers in environmentally sound agricultural production may be included in order to enhance their awareness of problems such as improper usage of fertilisers and pesticides which can pollute soil, water and air and indirectly endanger the community's health.

FDI in Large-Scale Agriculture: a foreign individual, company, trust or state that is engaged in large-scale agriculture and granted access and control over agricultural land-use rights or land ownership.

Foreign Direct Investment (FDI): an investment is termed FDI if the provider of capital is on one side of an international border while the delivery of goods or services occurs on the other and the capital provider also gains a degree of influence or control over the activities related to the delivery of goods or services.

Indigenous people: people who reside in certain parts of the country and live in their ancestral lands under a tribal system. They have their own indigenous languages which are used as the only languages or as their mother tongues.

They are distinct from other societies who are now prevailing in their territories. They are determined to preserve and transmit to future generations their ancestral territories and their ethnic identity.

Market Economy: an economic system whereby prices of goods and services are determined by the interaction of demand and supply. The market plays a huge role in making economic decisions, and there is little government intervention in comparison to the command economy.

Pro-poor FDI in Large-Scale Agriculture: FDI in large-scale agriculture but, in addition, the investment is designed to benefit the poor through (1) creation of employment for the locals by making the farming labour-intensive rather than capital-intensive; (2) improving working conditions such as wages, working hours, health insurance and other benefits; (3) increasing occupational health and safety standards of benefit to agricultural workers; (4) integrating local smallholder farmers with foreign investors; (5) improving host country's food security, especially those who are food deficit like Ethiopia, by increasing yield for their agricultural production; and (6) designing for allied local benefits such as road infrastructure, schools and health centres. In addition, pro-poor FDI in large-scale agriculture recognises and respects existing rights of individuals and/or communities in land and land-based resources and creates an environment in which the local communities participate in decision-making when leasing or selling the land and in the land development project cycle.

Social Infrastructure: a subset of the infrastructure sector and includes education, health, sanitation and water supply.

The terms *large-scale agriculture*, *large-scale farming* and *commercial farming* mean the same in this study and are used interchangeably.

The terms *the case studies* and *the agricultural investment projects* mean the same in this study and are used interchangeably.

The terms *regime* and *government* mean the same in this study and are used interchangeably.

The terms *indigenous people*, *local residents*, *villagers* and *community* mean the same in this study and are used interchangeably.

References

Aalen, L., (2002), *Ethnic federalism in a dominant party state: The Ethiopian experience 1991–2000*. Bergen: Chr. Michelsen Institute – Development Studies and Human Rights.

Abeasi, K., (2003), *Host country policies on FDI with particular reference to developing countries: A brief commentary. The development dimension of FDI: Policy and rule-making perspectives*. Proceedings of the Expert Meeting held in Geneva. UNCTAD/ITE/IIA/2003/4.

Adato, M., and Hoddinott, J., (2008), *Social protection: Opportunities for Africa*. IFPRI Policy Brief 5, September 2008. http://ebrary.ifpri.org/cdm/ref/collection/p15738coll2/id/12397, accessed on 27 July 2015.

AfDB, (2011), *Federal Democratic Republic of Ethiopia Country Strategy Paper 2011–2015*. Tunis: African Development Bank Group.

Allard, G., and Garot, M.J., (2010), The impact of the new labour law in China: New hiring strategies for foreign firms? *Revista Direito GV, SÃO PAULO*, Vol. 6, No. 2, pp. 527–540, July-December 2010, www.scielo.br/pdf/rdgv/v6n2/a09v6n2.pdf, accessed on 22 July 2015.

Alsan, M., Bloom, D.E., and Canning, D., (2004), *The effect of population health on foreign direct investment*. Cambridge, MA: National Bureau of Economic Research (NBER), Working Paper Series. www.nber.org/papers/w10596, accessed on 20 July 2015.

Amani, K., Nyange, D.A., Kweka, J.P., and Leyaro, V., (2003), *Trade policies and agricultural trade in the SADC region: Challenges and implications. Report for Food, Agriculture and Natural Resources Policy Network*. Dar es Salaam: Bank of Tanzania, Economic Bulletin, Various Issues, January 2003.

AMCOW, (2014), *Analysis of impacts of large-scale investments in agriculture on water resources, ecosystems and livelihoods; And development of policy options for decision makers. Summary of Initial Findings of the joint project of FAO, UNEP, GRiD-ARENDAL and IWMI*. Abuja: African Ministers' Council on Water.

Anyanwu, J.C., and Yameogo, D.N., (2015), *What drives foreign direct investments into West Africa? An empirical investigation*. Abidjan: African Development Bank, www.researchgate.net/publication/273499796_WHAT_DRIVES_FOREIGN_DIRECT_INVESTMENTS_INTO_WEST_AFRICA_AN_EMPIRICAL_INVESTIGATION, accessed on 21 July 2015.

Assosa University, (2015), *Benshanguel-Gumuz Regional State*, www.asu.edu.et/index.php?option=com_content&view=article&id=2&Itemid=60&lang=en, accessed on 3 June 2015.

Astatike, G., and Assefa, H., (2005), *Determin, ants of foreign direct investment in Ethiopia: A timeseries analysis*. Paper prepared for the 4th International Conference on the

Ethiopian Economy, June 2005, University of Westminster, London, www.wmin.ac.uk/westminsterresearch, accessed on 20 September 2015.

Athukorala, W., (2003), *The impact of Foreign direct investment for economic growth: A case study in Sri Lanka.* 9th International Conference on Sri Lanka Studies, Full Paper Number 092, Department of Economics, Faculty of Arts, University of Peradeniya, Sri Lanka.

Atkinson, M.M., and Coleman, W.D., (1989), *The state, business and industrial change in Canada.* Toronto: University of Toronto Press.

AU, (2008), *Social policy framework for Africa.* 1st Session of the AU Conference of Ministers in charge of Social Development, Windhoek, Namibia. African Union, www.au.int, accessed on 27 July 2015.

AUC-AfDB-UNECA, (2007), *Land policy in Africa: A framework to strengthen land rights, enhance productivity and secure livelihoods: Background document.* Addis Ababa, Ethiopia: AUC-AfDB-UNECA Joint Land Policy Initiative.

AUC-AfDB-UNECA, (2010), *Framework and guidelines on land policy in Africa.* Addis Ababa, Ethiopia: AUC-AfDB-UNECA Joint Land Policy Initiative.

AUC-AfDB-UNECA, (2011), *Concept note for the high level policy forum on land based FDI in Africa: Making investment work for African agricultural development* (Nairobi, October 2011). Addis Ababa, Ethiopia: UNECA.

AUC-AfDB-UNECA, (2014), *Guiding principles on large scale land based investments in Africa.* Addis Ababa, Ethiopia: AUC-AfDB-UNECA Joint Land Policy Initiative.

AU Assembly, (2009), *Declaration on land issues and challenges in Africa*, Assembly/AU/Decl.I (XIII) Rev.I, July 2009.

Balasubramanyam, V., (2003), *Host country FDI policies and development objectives. The development dimension of FDI: Policy and rule-making perspectives.* Proceedings of the Expert Meeting held in Geneva. UNCTAD/ITE/IIA/2003/4.

Balcha, B., (2007), *Restructuring state and society: Ethnic federalism in Ethiopia.* PhD Thesis, Aalborg University, Denmark.

Bandelj, N., (2001), *Culture, contacts and capital: Social relations as determinants of foreign direct investment in Central and Eastern Europe.* Proposal for the EPIC second cohort advance research workshop, http://citeseerx.ist.psu.edu/viewdoc/download?doi=10.1.1.198.879&rep=rep1&type=pdf, accessed on 27 July 2015.

Banga, R., (2003), *Impact of government policies and investment agreements on FDI inflows. Indian council for research on international economic relations.* Working Paper No. 116. New Delhi: Indian Council for Research on International Economic Relations (ICRIER).

Baniak, A., Cukrowski, J., and Herczynski, J., (2002), *On determinants of foreign direct investment in transition economies.* Praha 1, Czech Republic: Center for Economic Research and Graduate Education – Economics Institute. www.cergeei.cz/pdf/gdn/rrc/RRCII_41_paper_01.pdf, accessed on 27 July 2015.

Barrell, R., and Pain, N., (1996), An econometric analysis of U.S. Foreign direct investment. *The Review of Economics and Statistics*, Vol. 78, No. 2, pp. 200–207.

Bartels, F.L., Kratzsch, S., and Eicher, M., (2008), *Foreign direct investment in Sub-Saharan Africa: Determinants and location decision.* Research and Statistics Branch, Working Paper 08/2008. Vienna, Austria: UNIDO.

Basu, A., and Srinivasan, K., (2002), *Foreign direct investment in Africa – Some case studies.* IMF Working Paper, Washington, DC, WP/02/61, www.imf.org/external/pubs/ft/wp/2002/wp0261.pdf, accessed on 20 July 2015.

Berhanu, K., (n.d.), *Ethiopia: Beleaguered opposition under a dominant party system.* Addis Ababa, Ethiopia: Addis Ababa University.

Bhargava, A., (2001), *Nutrition, health, and economic development: Some policy priorities*. Commission on Macroeconomics and Health Working Paper Series WG1: 14. Geneva: World Health Organization,

Bissoon, O., (2011), *Can better institutions attract more foreign direct investment? Evidence from developing countries*. Kozani, Greece: International Conference on Applied Economics – ICOAE, Technological Educational Institute of Western Macedonia, http://kastoria.teikoz.gr/icoae2/wordpress/wp-content/uploads/2011/10/007.pdf, accessed on 28 July 2015.

Bloom, D.E., and Canning, D., (2000), The health and wealth of nations. *Science*, Vol. 287, No. 5456, pp. 1207–1209.

Bloom, D.E., and Canning, D., (2008), *Population health and economic growth*. Commission on Growth and Development. Working Paper No. 24, Washington, DC, http://siteresources.worldbank.org/EXTPREMNET/Resources/489960-1338997241035/Growth_Commission_Working_Paper_24_Population_Health_Economic_Growth.pdf.

Bloom, D.E., Canning, D., and Jamison, D.T., (2004), Health, wealth and welfare. *Journal of Finance and Development*, pp. 10–15, www.imf.org/external/pubs/ft/fandd/2004/03/pdf/bloom.pdf, accessed on 21 July 2015.

Blyde, J., Kugler, M., and Stein, E., (2004), *Exporting vs outsourcing by MNC subsidiaries: Which determines FDI spillovers?* Discussion Papers in Economics and Econometrics. Southampton: University of Southampton.

Boman, M., and Hellqvist, C., (2012), *Swedish FDI in Africa: Locational determinants of FDI from the perspective of the OLI paradigm*. Master Thesis, Department of Business Studies, Uppsala Universitet, Uppsala, Sweden, http://uu.diva-portal.org/smash/get/diva2:534466/FULLTEXT01.pdf, accessed on 7 July 2015.

Briassoulis, H., (2004), *Policy integration for complex policy problems: What, why and how*. Paper presented at the 2004 Berlin Conference on the Human Dimensions of the Global Environmental Change: Greening of policies – Interlinkages and policy integration, Berlin, Germany, December 3–4, 2004.

Briggs, P., (2013), *Ethiopia: The Bradt travel guide*. 3rd Edition. Chalfont St Peters: Bradt, 2002, p. 492.

Brown, L.R., (2013), *Food, fuel, and the global land grab*. The Futurist January-February 2013. Chicago, IL: World Future Society.

Buccus, I., Hemson, D., Hicks, J., and Piper, L., (2008), Community development and engagement with local governance in South Africa. *Oxford University Press and Community Development Journal*, Vol. 43, No. 3, pp. 297–311.

CGIAR, (2014), *Can foreign direct investment benefit smallholders and investors?* https://wle.cgiar.org/thrive/2014/07/22/can-foreign-direct-investment-benefit-smallholders-andinvestors, accessed on 14 May 2016.

Chari, V.V., (2004), Discussion of growth and foreign direct investment: Does policy play a role? *American Agricultural Economics Association*, pp. 802–804.

Cheung, K., and Lin, P., (2004), Spillover effects of FDI on innovation in China: Evidence from the provincial data. *Science Direct, China Economic Review*, Vol. 15, No. 2004, pp. 25–44, http://down.cenet.org.cn/upfile/56/200741293956148.pdf, accessed on 8 July 2015.

Clark, S.W., (2000), Tax incentives for Foreign direct investment: Empirical evidence on effects and alternative policy options. *Canadian Tax Journal*, Vol. 48, No. 4, pp. 1139–1180.

Cotula, L., (2012), The international political economy of the global land rush: A critical appraisal of trends, scale, geography and drivers. *The Journal of Peasant Studies*, Vol. 39, No. 3–4, pp. 649–680.

Cotula, L., and Vermeulen, S., (2009), Deal or no deal: The outlook for agricultural land investment in Africa. *The Royal Institute of International Affairs*, Vol. 85, No. 6, pp. 1233–1247.

Cotula, L., Vermeulen, S., Leonard, R., and Keeley, J., (2009), *Land grab or development opportunity? Agricultural investment and international land deals in Africa*. London/ Rome: IIED/FAO/IFAD. ISBN: 978-1-84369-741-1 C, http://pubs.iied.org/12561IIED.

Cox, E., (2010), *The landowner's guide to sustainable farm leasing*. Des Moines, IA: Drake University Agricultural Law Center, www.law.drake.edu/agLaw, accessed on 18 May 2015.

CSA, (2007), *Benshanguel-Gumuz regional state population density*. Addis Ababa, Ethiopia: Central Statistics Agency.

Cuffaro, N., and Hallam, D., (2011), *"Land grabbing" in developing countries: Foreign investors, regulation and codes of conduct*. Paper presented at the international conference on Global Land Grabbing, 6–8 April 2011, organised by the Land Deals Politics Initiative (LDPI) in collaboration with the Journal of Peasant Studies. www.future-agricultures.org/papers-andpresentations/conference-papers-2/1305-land-grabbing-in-developing-countries-foreigninvestors-regulation-and-codes-of-conduct/file, accessed on 13 November 2015.

Curry, N., (1993), Rural development in the 1990s – does prospect lie in retrospect? In Murray, M., & Greer, J. (eds), *Rural development in Ireland: A challenge for the 1990s*, pp. 21–39, Aldershot: Avebury.

Daude, C., Mazza, J., and Morrison, A., (2003), *Core labour standards and foreign direct investment in Latin America and the Caribbean: Does lax enforcement of labour standards attract investors?* www.ibrarian.net/navon/paper/CORE_LABOR_STAND ARDS_AND_FOREIGN_DIRECT_INVESTMEN.pdf?paperid=1232117, accessed on 22 July 2015.

Davies, R.B., and Vadlamannati, K.C., (2011), *A race to the bottom in labour standards? An empirical investigation*, www.etsg.org/ETSG2011/Papers/Chaitanya.pdf, accessed on 22 July 2015.

De Schutter, O., (2009), *Large-scale land acquisitions and leases: A set of core principles and measures to address the human rights challenge, UN Special Rapporteur on the right to food*. New York: United Nations.

De Schutter, O., (2011), How not to think of land-grabbing: Three critiques of large-scale investments in farmland. *The Journal of Peasants Studies*, Vol. 38, No. 2, pp. 249–279.

De Wit, P., and Verheye, W., (2009), Land use planning for sustainable development. *Land Use, Land Cover and Soil Sciences*, Vol. III, www.eolss.net/sample-chapters/c19/E1-05-03-01.pdf, accessed on 26 July 2015.

Demirhan, E., and Masca, M., (2008), Determinants of foreign direct investment flows to developing countries: A cross-sectional analysis. *Prague Economic Papers, University of Economics, Prague 2008*, Vol. 17, No. 4, pp. 356–369.

Devereux, S., and Sabates-Wheeler, R., (2004), *Transformative social protection*. Institute of Development Studies (IDS) Working Paper 232, Brighton, Sussex, www.unicef.org/ socialpolicy/files/Transformative_Social_Protection.pdf, accessed on 27 July 2015.

Djire, M., Keita, A., and Diawara, A., (2012), *Agricultural investments and land acquisitions in Mali: Context, trends and case studies*. London/Bamako: IIED/GERSDA.

Djurfeldt, A.A., (2012), African re-agrarianization? Accumulation or pro-poor agricultural growth? *World Development*, Vol. 41, pp. 217–231, Elsevier Ltd, Printed in Great Britain.

Dorward, A., Kydd, J., Morrison, J., and Urey, I., (2003), A policy agenda for pro-poor agricultural growth. *World Development*, Vol. 32, No. 1, pp. 73–89, Elsevier Ltd, Printed in Great Britain.

Dunning, J.H., (2000), The eclectic paradigm as an envelope for economic and business theories of MNE activity. *International Business Review*, Vol. 9, No. 2000, pp. 163–190, www. exeter.ac.uk/media/universityofexeter/internationalexeter/documents/iss/Dunning_ IBR_2000.pdf, accessed on 10 July 2015.

Dupasquier, C., and Osakwe, P.N., (2006), Foreign direct investment in Africa: Performance, challenges, and responsibilities. *Journal of Asian Economics*, Vol. 17, pp. 241–260.

EAILAA, (2014), *Status report on investment projects*. Addis Ababa, Ethiopia: Ethiopian Agricultural Investment Land Administration Agency, September 2014.

EC, (2006), *Land use planning guidelines*. European Commission, http://ec.europa.eu/ environment/seveso/pdf/landuseplanning_guidance_en.pdf, accessed on 26 July 2015.

EGP, (2016), *Ethiopian economy*. Addis Ababa, Ethiopia: Ethiopian Government Portal, www.ethiopia.gov.et/web/Pages/Economy, accessed on 14 May 2016.

Eguren, I.R., (2008), Moving up and down the ladder: Community-based participation in public dialogue and deliberation in Bolivia and Guatemala. *Oxford University Press and Community Development Journal*, Vol. 43, pp. 312–328.

Ekonomifakta, (2013), *Agricultural toward Industrial*, Online accessible: www.ekonomi fakta.se/en/Swedish-economic-history/Agricultural-toward-insutrial/, accessed on 18 August 2013.

Elibariki, M., (2007), *The impact of foreign direct investment on agricultural productivity and poverty reduction in Tanzania*. Japan: Kyoto University, Online accessible: http:// mpra.ub.unimuenchen. de/3671/, accessed on 15 October 2011.

Emery, J.T., Spence, M.T., Wells, L.T., and Buehrer, T., (2000), *Administrative barriers to foreign investment*. Reducing red tape in Africa, Foreign Investment Advisory Service, Occasional Paper, No. 14. The International Finance Corporation and the World Bank, Washington, DC, https://openknowledge.worldbank.org/bitstream/handle/10986/15192/ multi_page.pdf?sequence=1, accessed on 29 July 2015.

Essays, UK., (November 2013), *The national development policies of Ethiopia economics essay*, Nottingham, www.ukessays.com/essays/economics/the-national-development-policiesof-ethiopia-economics-essay.php?cref=1.

Esty, D., and Gentry, B., (1997), *Foreign investment, globalisation and the environment. Globalisation and the environment*. Paris: OECD.

ETA, (2015), *Distances from the capital city to various regions of Ethiopia*. Addis Ababa, Ethiopia: Ethiopian Transport Authority.

Ethiopian Treasures, (2015), *The Derg (1974–1991)*, www.ethiopiantreasures.co.uk/pages/ derg.htm, accessed on 13 September 2015.

ETIA, (2013), *An investment guide to Ethiopia: Opportunities and conditions*, Addis Ababa, Ethiopia: Ethiopian Investment Agency.

Fan, E.X., (2002), *Technological spillovers from Foreign direct investment – A survey*. ERD Working Paper Series No. 33, Economic and Research Department. Asian Development Bank, Manila, ISSN 1655–5252, www.adb.org/sites/default/files/publication/28326/ wp033.pdf, accessed on 8 July 2015.

FAO, (1993a), *Land use planning guidelines*, www.mpl.ird.fr/crea/tallercolombia/FAO/ AGLL/pdfdocs/guidelup.pdf, accessed on 26 July 2015.

FAO, (1993b), *The state of food and agriculture – Ethiopia*. Rome: Economic and Social Development Department.

FAO, (1995), *Environmental impact assessment of irrigation and drainage projects*. FAO irrigation and drainage paper 53, Rome, ftp://ftp.fao.org/agl/aglw/Morini/05_EIA.pdf, accessed on 25 July 2015.

FAO, (2001), *Agricultural investment & productivity in developing countries. Economic and Social Development Department.* Rome, Italy: Food and Agriculture Organization of the United Nations, www.fao.org/docrep/003/x9447e/x9447e03.htm#TopOfPage, accessed on 3 November 2011.

FAO, (2004), *FAO land tenure notes: Leasing agricultural land.* Rome, Italy: Food and Agriculture Organization of the United Nations, www.fao.org/3/a-y5513e.pdf, accessed on 18 May 2015.

FAO, (2009), *Foreign direct investment: Win-win or land grab? Policy brief, World summit on Food Security.* Rome, Italy: Food and Agriculture Organization of the United Nations, 16–18 November 2009.

FAO, (2012), *Voluntary guidelines on the responsible governance of tenure of land, fisheries and forests in the context of national food security.* Rome, Italy: Food and Agriculture Organization of the United Nations, 2012.

Financial Times, (2008), *Daewoo to cultivate Madagascar land for free.* November 19, 2008, https://www.ft.com/content/6e894c6a-b65c-11dd-89dd-0000779fd18c, accessed on 16 February 2012

Fiszbein, A., (1997), The emergence of local capacity: Lessons from Colombia. *World Development*, Vol. 25, No. 7, pp. 1029–1043.

Foster, V., and Morella, E., (2011), *Ethiopia's infrastructure, a continental perspective.* Policy Research Working Paper. WPS5595. The World Bank, African Region, Sustainable Development Department, Washington, DC, http://wwwds. worldbank.org/external/default/WDSContentServer/WDSP/IB/2011/03/17/000158349_2011_0317130811/Rendered/PDF/WPS5595.pdf, accessed on 21 July 2015.

GAO, (1990), *Report on the furniture finishing industry.* Washington, DC: Government Accountability Office.

Gazdar, H., and Quan, J., (2004), *Poverty and access to land in South Asia.* London: DFID.

Geda, A., (2006), *The political economy of growth in Ethiopia,* Chapter 4, Vol. 2, http://alemayehu.com/AA%20Recent%20Publication/Growth_CambChap_Sept2006.pdf, accessed on 15 September 2015.

Gentry, B., (1999), *Foreign direct investment and the environment: Boon or bane?,* Background Paper for the OECD Conference on Foreign Direct investment and the Environment. Paris.

Gerlach, A.C., and Liu, P., (2010), *Resource-seeking foreign direct investment in African agriculture: A review of country case studies.* Rome, Italy: Food and Agriculture Organization of the United Nations.

Gish, S., Thay, W., and Latif, Z.A., (2007), *Cultures of the world: Ethiopia.* 2nd Edition. Tarrytown, NY: Times, United States.

GIZ, (2012), *Land use planning: Concepts, tools and applications,* www.giz.de/expertise/downloads/Fachexpertise/giz2012-en-land-use-planning-manual.pdf, accessed on 24 July 2015.

Global Policy Forum, (2012), *The 21st century African land rush. Social and economic policy/hunger,* www.globalpolicy.org/component/content/article/217-hunger/51289-the-21stcentury-african-land-rush.html, accessed on 4 February 2013.

Globerman, S., and Chen, Z., (2010), *Best policy practices for promoting inward and outward Foreign direct investment. Trade, investment policy and international cooperation.* Ottawa, ON: The Conference Board of Canada. Canada Report October 2010.

Gordon, K., and Pohl, J., (2010), *Freedom of investment process: Responsible investment in Agriculture. 12th OECD Roundtable on Freedom of Investment.* Paris: Organization for Economic Co-operation and Development (OECD), Online accessible: www.oecd.org/daf/investment, accessed on 14 June 2012.

Görgen, M., Rudloff, B., Simons, J., Üllenberg, A., Väth, S., and Wimmer, L., (2009), *Foreign direct investment in land in developing countries.* Division 45, Agriculture, Fisheries and Food. Eschborn (December 2009), GTZ, Federal Ministry for Economic Cooperation and Development.

Gow, H.R., Streeter, D.H., and Swinnen, J.F.M., (2000), How private contract enforcement mechanisms can succeed where public institution fail: The case of Juhocukoras. *Agricultural Economics*, Vol. 23, pp. 253–265.

GRARDB, (2015), *Agricultural projects' status report.* Addis Ababa, Ethiopia: Gambella Regional Agricultural and Rural Development Bureau.

Graymore, D., (2003), Corporate social responsibility and FDI. *UNCTAD/ITE/IIA/2003/4, Part III – Corporate Social Responsibility*, pp. 173–185.

Grimm, M., Klasen, S., and McKay, A., (2007), *Determinants of pro-poor growth: Analytical issues and findings from country cases.* London: Palgrave Macmillan UK.

Groh, A.P., and Wich, M., (2009), *A composite measure to determine a host country's attractiveness for foreign direct investment.* IESE Business School, University of Navarra, Barcelona, Working Paper, WP-833, November 2009.

Guba, E., and Lincoln, Y., (1981), *Effective evaluation.* San Francisco: Jossey-Bass.

Haaland, J.I., and Wooton, I., (1999), International competition for multinational investment. *Scandinavian Journal of Economics*, Vol. 101, No. 4, pp. 631–649.

Hailu, Z.A., (2010), Impact of Foreign direct investment on trade of African countries. *International Journal of Economics and Finance*, Vol. 2, No. 3, pp. 122–133, August 2010, www.ccsenet.org/journal/index.php/ijef/article/viewFile/5393/5340, accessed on 21 July 2015.

Hallam, D., (2009), *Foreign investment in developing country agriculture – Issues, policy implications and international response. Global Forum VIII on International Investment.* Paris: Organization for Economic Co-operation and Development (OECD).

Hamel, J., (1993), *Case study methods. Qualitative research methods.* Vol. 32. Thousand Oaks, CA: Sage.

Hanstad, T., Nielsen, R., and Brown, J., (2004), *Lands and livelihoods: Making land rights real for India's rural poor.* FAO Livelihoods System programme Paper, FAO, Rome, Italy, 2004.

Henze, P.B., (2000), *Layers of time: A history of Ethiopia.* London: Palgrave Macmillan UK.

HoA-REC/N, (2012), *Sustainable development of the Gambella and Rift Valley landscapes.* Addis Ababa, Ethiopia: Horn of Africa Regional Environment Centre and Network.

Hough, J., and Neuland, E.W., (2000), *Global business environments and strategies. Managing for global competitive advantage.* 1st Edition. Southern Africa, Cape Town: Oxford University Press.

IEG, (1962), *Second five year development plan 1963–67.* Addis Ababa, Ethiopia: Imperial Ethiopian Government, October 1962.

IOM, (2014), *Impact of private investment on natural disasters in Gambella Region of Ethiopia.* Addis Ababa, Ethiopia: International Organization for Migration.

Ireland's Department of Jobs, Enterprise and Innovation, (2014), *Policy statement on Foreign direct investment in Ireland*, www.djei.ie/publications/enterprise/2014/Policy_Statement_FDI_Ireland_July_2014.pdf, accessed on 8 July 2015.

Irvin, R.A., and Stansbury, J., (2004), Citizen participation in decision making: Is it worth the effort? *Public Administration Review*, Vol. 64, No. 1.

Janicki, H.P., and Wunnava, P.V., (2004), Determinants of foreign direct investment: Empirical evidence from EU accession candidates. *Applied Economics*, Vol. 36, pp. 505–509.

Javorcik, B.S., and Spatareanu, M., (2005), *Do foreign investors care about labour market regulations?* Washington, DC: World Bank, http://andromeda.rutgers.edu/~marianas/publications/Do%20Foreign%20Investors%20Care%20about%20Labor%20Market%20Regulations.pdf, accessed on 22 July 2015.

Jenkin, S., (2011), *Foreign investment in agriculture: A medium-term perspective in Zambia.* 4th European Conference on African Studies, Uppsala, 15–18 June 2011.

Jha, V., Markandya, A., and Vossenaar, R., (1999), *Reconciling trade and the environment: Lessons from case studies in developing countries.* Cheltenham, UK: Edward Elgar Publishing Ltd.

Jimenez, A., (2011), Political risk as determinant of Southern European FDI in neighbouring developing countries. *Emerging Markets Finance & Trade*, Vol. 47, No. 4, pp. 59–74.

Kakwani, N., and Pernia, E.M., (2000), What is pro-poor growth? *Asian Development Bank, Studies of Asian and Pacific Economic Issues*, Vol. 18, No. 1, pp. 1–16.

Karlsson, J., (2012), *What have different actors done to increase the benefits of commercial agriculture investments for poor people?* Stockholm: Swedish International Development Cooperation Agency, http://sidaenvironmenthelpdesk.se/wordpress3/wpcontent/uploads/2013/04/Increased-benefits-of-commersical-agriculture-investmenst-for-poor people1.pdf, accessed on 19 July 2015.

Kefale, A., (2009), *Federalism and ethnic conflict in Ethiopia: A comparative regional study.* Abingdon: Routledge Series in Federal Studies.

Kikula, I.A., Kauzeni, A.S., Mohamed, S.A., and Lyimo, J.G., (1993), *Land use planning and resource assessment in Tanzania: A case study.* IIED Environmental Planning Issues No. 3, IRA Research Paper No. 35, London, http://pubs.iied.org/pdfs/7751IIED.pdf, accessed on 26 July 2015.

Killing, J.P., (1983), *Strategies for joint venture success.* Vol. 22. New York: Routledge.

Kim, A.M., (2011), *The impact of Foreign Direct Investments (FDIs) on Economic Growth and Development in Kenya.* Nairobi: University of Nairobi, www.aibuma.org/proceedings 2011/aibuma2011_submission_7.pdf, accessed on 3 November 2011.

Kim, K.R., (2003), South Korea's inward foreign direct investment: Policy and environment. *Recalibrating the U.S. – Republic of Korea Alliance*, Chapter 11, pp. 207–220.

Klapsis, A., (2014), *Economic crisis and political extremism in Europe: From the 1930s to the present.* Brussels: Wilfred Martens Centre for European Studies 2014, www.academia.edu, accessed on 16 September 2015.

Klavens, J., and Zamparutti, A., (1995), *Foreign direct investment and environment in central and Eastern Europe: A survey.* Washington, DC: World Bank.

Kokko, A., (2003), *Globalization and FDI policies. The development dimension of FDI: Policy and rule-making perspectives.* Proceedings of the Expert Meeting held in Geneva, UNCTAD/ITE/IIA/2003/4.

Krueger, J., Gebru, A.K., and Asnake, I., (2012), Environmental permitting in Ethiopia: No restraint on "Unstoppable Growth?" *Haramaya Law Review*, Vol. 1, No. 1, pp. 73–102.

Kucera, D., (2001), *The effects of core workers' rights on labour costs and foreign direct investment: Evaluating the "Conventional Wisdom".* Discussion Paper, International Institute for Labour Studies, Geneva, http://natlex.ilo.ch/wcmsp5/groups/public/ – dgreports/ – inst/documents/publication/wcms_193670.pdf, accessed on 22 July 2015.

Kumar, N., (2003), *Use and effectiveness of performance requirements: What can be learnt from the experiences of developed and developing countries? The development dimension of FDI: Policy and rule-making perspectives.* Proceedings of the Expert Meeting held in Geneva, UNCTAD/ITE/IIA/2003/4.

Lall, S., (2000), *FDI and development: Research issues in the emerging context*. Policy Discussion Paper No. 0020, Centre for International Economic Studies, University of Adelaide, Adelaide.

Land for Good Organisation, (2012), *A landowner's guide to leasing land for farming. The Land Access Project*. Keene: Land for Good Organisation, www.landforgood.org, accessed on 18 May 2015.

Leykun, M., (2013), Ethiopian privatization agency to transfer 20 state owned enterprises. *Fortune Report*, 26 August 2013. Addis Ababa, Ethiopia: Addis Fortune.

Lipsey, R.E., (1999), *The role of direct investment in international capital flows*. M. Feldstein, ed. Chicago: University of Chicago Press.

Liu, P., (2004), *Impacts of Foreign agricultural investment on developing countries: Evidence from case studies*. FAO Commodity and Trade Policy Research Working Paper No. 47, Rome.

Lobao, L., and Meyer, K., (2001), The great agricultural transition, change, and social consequences of twentieth century US farming. *Annual Review of Sociology*, Vol. 27, pp. 103–124, Annual Reviews.

Lobao, L., and Stofferahn, C.W., (2008), The community effects of industrialized farming: Social science research and challenges to corporate farming laws. *Agriculture and Human Values*, Vol. 25, pp. 219–240.

Loewendahl, H., (2001), A framework for FDI promotion. *Transnational Corporation*, Vol. 10, No. 1 (April 2001), www.investmentmap.org/docs/fdi-2547.pdf, accessed on 29 July 2015.

Lohani, B.N, Evans, J.W., Everitt, R.R., Ludwig, H.L., Carpenter, R.A., and Tu, S.L., (1997), *Environmental impact assessment for developing countries in Asia, Vol. I – Overview*, Asian Development Bank, Manila, www.adb.org/sites/default/files/publication/29779/eia-developing-countries-asia.pdf, accessed on 25 July 2015.

Lu, H., and Huang, H., (2008), Dirty industry migration globally and to China – An empirical study. *International Review of Business Research Papers*, Vol. 4, No. 2, pp. 176–202, www.bizresearchpapers.com/Paper-13.pdf, accessed on 26 July 2015.

Luo, Y., (2002), Contract, cooperation, and performance in international joint ventures. *Strategic Management Journal*, Vol. 23, pp. 903–919.

Lv, L., Wen, S., and Xiong, Q., (2010), Determinants and performance index of foreign direct investment in China's agriculture. *China Agricultural Economic Review*, Vol. 2, No. 1, pp. 36–48.

Lyakurwa, W., (2009), Prospects for economic governance: Resilient pro-poor growth. *Foresight*, Vol. 11, No. 4, pp. 66–81. Bingley: Emerald Group Publishing Limited.

Mabesa, M., and Whittal, J., (2011), *Analysis of the current cadastral system in Lesotho using Viable Systems Modeling (VSM)*. University of Cape Town, AfricaGEO 2011, Online accessible: http://africageodownloads.info/6a_096_%20mabesa_whittal.pdf, (accessed on 20 September 2012).

Mabey, N., and McNally, R., (1999), *Foreign direct investment and the environment: From pollution havens to sustainable development*. Surrey: WWF-UK, www.oecd.org/investment/mne/2089912.pdf, accessed on 26 July 2015.

Majeed, M.T., and Ahmad, E., (2008), Human capital development and FDI in developing countries. *Journal of Economic Cooperation*, Vol. 29, No. 3, pp. 79–104.

Majumdar, D., (2006), Collaboration among government agencies with special reference to New Zealand: A literature review. *Social Policy Journal of New Zealand*, No. 27, pp. 183–198.

Masaba, C.M., Verkuijl, H., Ba, I., Marini, A., Serpagli, A., Liversage, H., and Jonckheere, S., (2013), *Securing livelihoods, land and natural resource rights through inclusive business models: Lessons from Uganda and Mali.* Annual World Bank Conference on land and Poverty, World Bank, Washington, DC, April 8–11, 2013.

Meijers, E., and Stead, D., (2004), *Policy integration: What does it mean and how can it be achieved? A multi-disciplinary review.* Paper presented at the 2004 Berlin Conference on the Human Dimensions of the Global Environmental Change: Greening of policies – Interlinkages and policy integration, Berlin, December 3–4, 2004.

Mengistu, B., and Adams, S., (2007), Foreign direct investment, governance and economic development in developing countries. *Journal of Social, Political and Economic Studies,* Vol. 32, No. 2, pp. 223–249.

Metcalfe, S., and Kepe, T., (2008), Dealing land in the midst of poverty: Commercial Access to communal land in Zambia. *African and Asian Studies,* Vol. 7, pp. 235–257.

MoFED, UNDP, and UNCDF, (2007), *Emerging regions development programme in Ethiopia 2007–2011.* Addis Ababa, Ethiopia: MoFED.

Moline, D.J., (1993), A comment on whether Maquiladoras are in Mexico for low wages or to avoid pollution abatement costs. *Journal of Environment and Development,* Vol. 2, No. 1, pp. 221–241.

Moosa, I.A., (2002), *Foreign direct investment: Theory, evidence and practice.* London: Palgrave Macmillan.

Moreda, T., (2013), *Postponed local concerns: Implication of land acquisitions for Indigenous local communities in Benshanguel-Gumuz Regional State, Ethiopia.* Land Deals Politics Initiatives. Rotterdam: International Institute for Social Studies, Erasmus University.

Mutangadura, G., (2009), *A review of social protection experiences in Africa.* Draft paper. Save the Children, Save the Children, Sweden, http://resourcecentre.savethechildren.se/authors/mutangadura-g, accessed on 27 July 2015.

Nayak, D., and Choudhury, N.R., (2014), *A selective review of foreign direct investment theories.* ARTNeT Working Paper Series No. 143, March 2014, Bangkok, ESCAP, www.unescap.org/sites/default/files/AWP%20No.%20143.pdf, accessed on 1 June 2016.

Ndikumana, L., and Verick, S., (2007), *The linkages between FDI and domestic investment: Unravelling the developmental impact of Foreign investment in Sub-Saharan Africa.* University of Massachusetts, Economics Department, Cambridge, MA, Working paper Series. Paper 25, http://scholarworks.umass.edu/econ_workingpaper/25/, accessed on 27 November 2012.

Noorbakhsh, F., Paloni, A., and Youssef, A., (2001), Human capital and FDI inflows to developing countries: New empirical evidence. *World Development,* Vol. 29, No. 9, pp. 1593–1610.

Nordström, H., and Vaughan, S., (1999), *Trade and environment. Special Studies No. 4.* Geneva: World Trade Organization, www.wto.org/english/res_e/booksp_e/special_study_4_e.pdf, accessed on 26 July 2015.

North, D.C., (1990), *Institutions, institutional change and economic performance.* Cambridge: Cambridge University Press.

NPC, FDRE, (2016), *Growth and transformation plan II (GTP II) (2015/16–2019/20). Vol. I Main Text.* Addis Ababa, Ethiopia: NPC.

Oakland Institute, (2011), *Why you should care about land grabs,* http://media.oakland institute.org/why-you-should-care-about-land-grabs, accessed on 1 November 2011.

OECD, (2002a), *Foreign direct investment for development: Maximising benefits, minimizing costs.* Overview, Paris, www.oecd.org/investment/investmentfordevelop ment/1959815.pdf, accessed on 22 July 2015.

OECD, (2002b), *Environmental issues in policy-based competition for investment: A literature review.* Working party on global and structural policies, Environment Directorate,

Environment Policy Committee, Paris, www.oecd.org/officialdocuments/publicdisplaydoc umentpdf/?doclanguage=en&cote=env/epoc/gsp (2001)11/final, accessed on 25 July 2015.

Olney, W.W., (2013), *A race to the bottom? Employment protection and foreign direct investment*. Williamstown: Department of Economics, Williams College, http://web. williams.edu/Economics/wp/OlneyEmploymentProtectionAndFDI.pdf, accessed on 22 July 2015.

Persson, A., (2009), *Beyond the rhetoric: Mainstreaming environmental issues into poverty reduction strategies – The case of Ethiopia*. Saarbrücken: Lambert Academic Publishing.

Photius, (2015), *Ethiopia agriculture, the library of congress country studies; CIA World Factbook.* Fairfax, VA: Central Intelligence Agency, www.photius.com/countries/ethiopia/ economy/ethiopia_economy_agriculture.html, accessed on 6 October 2015.

Picciotto, S., (1999), Introduction: What rules for the world economy? In Picciotto, S. & Mayne, R. (eds), *Regulating international business: Beyond liberalization*, pp. 1–28. London: Palgrave Macmillan, www.palgrave.com/resources/sample-chapters/ 9780333776773_sample.pdf, accessed on 27 July 2015.

Picciotto, S., (2003), Corporate social responsibility for international business. *UNCTAD/ ITE/IIA/2003/4, Part III – Corporate Social Responsibility*, pp. 151–172.

Popovici, O.C., and Călin, A.C., (2014), FDI theories: A location-based approach. *The Romanian Economic Journal*, Vol. XVII, No. 53, pp. 3–24.

PPESA, (2014), *Privatization and Public Enterprises Supervising Agency*, www.ppesa. gov.et/?q=node/4, Accessed on 16 December 2015.

Quisumbing, A.R., (1994), *Improving women's agricultural productivity as farmers and workers*. World Bank, Education and Social Policy Department, ESP Discussion Paper Series No. 37, Washington, DC.

Rahmato, D., (2011), *Land to investors: Large-scale land transfers in Ethiopia*. Addis Ababa, Ethiopia: Forum for Social Studies.

Redea, M., (2009), *Employment and law. Teaching material*. Addis Ababa, Ethiopia: Justice and Legal System Research Institute, https://chilot.files.wordpress.com/2011/06/ employement-and-labour-law.pdf, accessed on 22 July 2015.

Revesz, R., (1994), Rehabilitating interstate competition: Rethinking the "Race to the Bottom" rational for federal environmental regulation. *New York University School of Law Review*. Vol. 67, p. 1210.

Robson, C., (1993), *Real world research: A resource for social scientists and practitioner – researchers*. Oxford: Blackwell Publishing.

Rodriguez, X.A., and Pallas, J., (2008), *Determinants of Foreign direct investment in Spain*. Galicia, Spain: Department of Quantitative Economics, University of Santiago de Compostela.

Ruffeis, D., Loiskandl, W., Awulachew, S.B., and Boelee, E., (2010), Evaluation of the environmental policy and impact assessment process in Ethiopia. *Impact Assessment and Project Appraisal*, Vol. 28, No. 1, pp. 29–40, http://dx.doi.org/10.3152/146155110X488844, accessed on 24 July 2015.

Ruger, J.P., Jamison, D.T., Bloom, D.E., and Canning, D., (2011), *Health and the economy. 3rd Edition, Chapter 15, global health: Diseases, programs, systems and policies*, Philadelphia, PA: University of Pennsylvania – School of Social Policy & Practice.

Sarna, R., (2005), *The impact of core labour standards on foreign direct investment in East Asia*, Tokyo: The Japan Institute for Labour Policy and Training, www.jil.go.jp/profile/ documents/Sarna.pdf, accessed on 22 July 2015.

Sass, M., (2003), *The effectiveness of host country policy measures in attracting FDI: The case of Hungary. The development dimension of FDI: Policy and rule-making perspectives.* Proceedings of the Expert Meeting held in Geneva, UNCTAD/ITE/IIA/2003/4.

Schüpbach, J.M., (2014), *Foreign direct investment in agriculture. The impact of outgrower schemes and large-scale farm employment on economic well-being in Zambia.* PhD Thesis, University of Zurich, Zurich.

Seyoum, B., (2009), Formal institutions and Foreign direct investment. *Thunderbird International Business Review*, Vol. 51, No. 2, pp. 165–181.

Shete, M., (2011), *Implications of land deals to livelihood security and natural resource management in Benshanguel Gumuz Regional State, Ethiopia.* Paper presented at the International Conference on Global Land Grabbing, Institute of Development Studies, University of Sussex, Sussex, April 6–8, 2011.

Stake, R.E., (2005), Qualitative case studies. In Denzin, N.K. & Lincoln, Y.S. (eds), *The Sage handbook of qualitative research*, 3rd Edition, pp. 443–466, Thousand Oaks, CA: Sage.

Steve, F., (2011), Africa for sale – Land and water grabs spell disaster for rural people and river. *International Rivers*, Vol. 26, No. 3.

Storey, D., (1999), Issues of integration, participation and empowerment in rural development: The case of leader in the Republic of Ireland. *Journal of Rural Studies*, Vol. 15, No. 3, pp. 307–315.

Tandon, A., (2005), *Population health and foreign direct investment: Does poor health signal poor government effectiveness?* Manilla: Economic and Research Department of Asian Development Bank, Policy Brief, Series No. 33, www.adb.org/sites/default/files/publication/28093/pb033.pdf, accessed on 21 July 2015.

Taylor, C.T., (2000), The impact of host country Government policy on US multinational investment decisions. *The World Economy*, Vol. 23, No. 5, pp. 635–647.

Tesfaye, M., (2008), *Environmental policy and laws of Ethiopia and clean fuel.* Nairobi: United Nations Environment Programme, www.unep.org/transport/pcfv/pdf/Ethiopia-EnvironmentalPolicy&CleanFuel.pdf, accessed on 24 July 2015.

Teshome, B.W., and Záhořík, J., (2008), Federalism in Africa: The case of ethnic-based federalism in Ethiopia. *International Journal of Human Sciences*, Vol. 5, Issue No. 2, pp. 1–39.

TeVelde, D.W., (2001), *Government policies towards inward foreign direct investment in developing countries: Implications for human capital formation and income inequality.* FDI, Human Capital and Education in Developing Countries, Technical Meeting, OECD, Paris, December 13–14, 2001.

Thabrew, L., Wiek, A., and Ries, R., (2009), Environmental decision making in multi-stakeholder contexts: Applicability of life cycle thinking in development planning and implementation. *Journal of Cleaner Production*, Vol. 17, pp. 67–76.

The Economist, (2013), *Labour standards: Racing to the bottom*, November 27, 2013, www.economist.com/blogs/freeexchange/2013/11/labour-standards, accessed on 22 July 2015.

Timmer, C.P., (1988), The agricultural transformation. *Handbook of Development Economics*, Vol. I, Elsevier Science Publishers B.V.

Todaro, M.P., (2000), *Economic development.* 7th Edition. Boston: Addison Wesley Longman.

Tran-Nguyen, A., (2010), *Global land grabbing: Issues and solutions.* Bern: Brot Fuer Alle, www.brotfueralle.ch/fileadmin/deutsch/2_Entwicklungpolitik_allgemein/A_Recht_auf_Na hrung/Global%20land%20grabbing%20by%20ATN.pdf, accessed on 19 July 2015.

Trink, M., (2007), *The role of investment promotion agencies at attracting foreign direct investment and their impact of economic development in central Europe.* The Czech Republic and Slovakia in Comparative Perspective. Budapest: Department of International Relations and European Studies, Central European University, http://diplomovka. sme.sk/zdroj/3122.pdf, accessed on 29 July 2015.

Tsakok, I., (2011), *Success in agricultural transformation – what it means and what makes it happen.* 1st Edition. Cambridge: Cambridge University Press.

TUAC, (1995), *Foreign direct investments and labour standards.* TUAC discussion paper for consultations with the OECD Committee on International Investment and Multinational Enterprises, December 13, TUAC Archives, Paris, www.tuac.org/en/public/doc/ papers/index.phtml, accessed on 22 July 2015.

Turner, J.W., (1993), *Ethiopia: A country study.* Washington, DC: Federal Research Division of the Library of Congress, Area Handbook Series..

UN, (2014), *Article on Social Protection Policy of Ethiopia. Delivering as one, One-UN programme of Ethiopia.* Addis Ababa, Ethiopia: United Nations, www.unicef.org/ethiopia, accessed on 27 July 2015.

UNCTAD, (1993), *World investment report 1993.* Geneva: Transnational Corporations and Integrated International Production. http://unctad.org/en/Docs/wir1993_en.pdf, accessed on 26 July 2015.

UNCTAD, (2009), *World investment report: Transnational corporations, agricultural production and development.* Geneva: United Nations Conference on Trade & Development, (UNCTAD), Online accessible: www.unctad.org/en/docs/wir2009_en.pdf, accessed on 3 November 2011.

UNECA, (2006), *Land policy in Africa: A framework of action to secure land rights, enhance productivity and secure livelihoods.* Issues Paper presented at the consultative workshop in March 2006, Addis Ababa, Ethiopia, www.uneca.org/sdd/meetings/Land Policy/IssuesPaper.pdf, accessed on 3 November 2011.

UNEP, (2004), *Environmental impact assessment and strategic environmental assessment: Towards an integrated approach*, Nairobi: United Nations Environment Programme, www.unep.ch/etu/publications/textONUbr.pdf, accessed on 24 July 2015.

Van Beers, C., and Van Den Bergh, J.C., (1997), An empirical multi-country analysis of the impact of environmental regulations on Foreign trade flows. *International Review for Social Sciences, KYKLOS*, Vol. 50, pp. 29–46.

Warner, M., (1999), Which way now? Choices for mainstreaming 'public involvement' in economic infrastructure projects in developing countries. *Development Policy Review*, Vol. 17, pp. 115–139.

Whittal, J., (2008), *Fiscal cadastral systems reform. A case study of the general valuation project 2000 in the city of Cape Town.* Calgary: Department of Geomatics, University of Calgary, UCGE Reports Number 20272, www.geomatics.ucalgary.ca/research/publica tions/GradTheses.html, accessed on 20 September 2012.

WHO, (2001), *Macroeconomics and health: Investing in health for economic development. Commission on macroeconomics and health.* Geneva: World Health Organization.

WHO, (2003), *Administrative map of Ethiopia.* Brazzaville: WHO Ethiopia Country Office. World health Organization Regional Office for Africa, www.afro.who.int/en/ ethiopia/who-country-office-ethiopia.html, accessed on 15 November 2015.

Williams, T.O., (2012), *FDI in agricultural land and investment in small-scale agricultural water management solutions: Incompatible models or a win-win combination for Africa?* Colombo: International Water Management Institute. Water for a food-secure world, Online accessible: www.waterenergy-food.org/ . . . /nexus_williams_fdi_in_ agriculture.pdf, accessed on 29 October 2013.

Williamson, O.E., (1979), Transaction-cost economics: The governance of contractual relations. *Journal of Law and Economics*, Vol. 22, No. 2, pp. 233–261.

World Bank, (2016), *Ethiopia's great run – The growth acceleration and how to pace it*. Washington, DC: World Bank Group. http://documents.worldbank.org/curated/en/693561467988949839/pdf/99399-REVISED-PUBLIC-thiopia-Economic-Update-2-11-16-web.pdf, accessed on 11 November 2016.

World Bank, (2010), *Rising global interest in Farmland. Can it yield sustainable and equitable Benefits?* Report of September 7, 2010. Washington, DC: World Bank Group, worldbank.org/external/default/WDSContentServer/WDSP/IB/2001/03/20/000094946_0103.

Worldometers, (2015), *Ethiopian population (1950–2014)*. The Worldometers, online platform, www.worldometers.info/world-population/ethiopia-population/, accessed on 5 October 2015.

Yassin, A., (2014), *Transnational large scale agricultural firms in Gambella regional state, Ethiopia: Local potentials, opportunities and constraints for market linkage and contractual farming schemes*. Future Agricultures. Sussex: Consortium Secretariat, Institute of Development Studies, University of Sussex.

Yen, N.T.K., and Luong, P.V., (2008), Participatory village and commune development planning (VDP/CDP) and its contribution to local community development in Vietnam. *Community Development Journal*, Vol. 43, No. 3, pp. 329–340.

Yin, R.K., (1994), *Case study research: Design and methods*. 2nd Edition. Thousand Oaks, CA: Sage.

Yin, R.K., (2003), *Case study research: Design and methods. 3rd Edition. Applied social research methods series*. Vol. 5, p. 13. Thousand Oaks, CA: Sage.

Zampini, D., (2008), *Developing a balanced framework for foreign direct investment in SADC: A decent work perspective*. Sankt Augustin, Germany: Konrad Adenauer Stiftung, www.kas.de/upload/auslandshomepages/namibia/MRI2008/MRI2008_05_Zampini.pdf, accessed on 22 July 2015.

Zarsky, L., (1999), *Havens, Halos and Spaghetti: Untangling the evidence about FDI and the environment*. Paris: Foreign Direct Investment and the Environment, OECD.

Zenawi, M., (2010), *Regulation by the council of ministers on the administration of agricultural investment land under the appointment of regions*. Addis Ababa, Ethiopia: Prime Minister of the Federal Democratic Republic of Ethiopia.

Policies and strategies

EPA (Environmental Protection Authority), (1997), Environmental Policy, Federal Democratic Republic of Ethiopia, Environmental Protection Authority, Addis Ababa, Ethiopia.

EPA, (2011), Ethiopia's climate Resilient Green Economy Strategy, Federal Democratic Republic of Ethiopia, Environmental Protection Authority, Addis Ababa, Ethiopia.

MoA, (2010), Guideline to prepare project documents on environmental impact assessment for agricultural investment, Ministry of Agriculture, Addis Ababa, April 2010

MoE (Ministry of Education), (1994), Education and Training Policy, Federal Democratic Republic Government of Ethiopia, Ministry of Education, Addis Ababa, Ethiopia, April 1994.

MoE, (2008), National Adult Education Strategy, Federal Democratic Republic Government of Ethiopia, Ministry of Education, Addis Ababa, Ethiopia, February 2008.

MoFED, (2003), Rural Development Policy and Strategies. Government of the Federal Democratic Republic of Ethiopia, Ministry of Finance and Economic Development, Economic Policy and Planning Department, Addis Ababa, Ethiopia, April 2003.

MoFED, (2010), Growth and Transformation Plan, Government of the Federal Democratic Republic of Ethiopia, Ministry of Finance and Economic Development, Addis Ababa, Ethiopia, September 2010.

MoH (Ministry of Health), (1993), Health Policy and Strategies, Transitional Government of Ethiopia, Ministry of Health, Addis Ababa, Ethiopia, September 1993.

MoI, (1941), Development in Ethiopia 1941–1964, Ministry of Information, The Imperial Ethiopian Government, 1941, Addis Ababa, Ethiopia.

MoI, (1964b), Development in Ethiopia 1941–1964, Ministry of Information, The Imperial Ethiopian Government, 1964, Addis Ababa, Ethiopia.

MoI, (1964a), Agriculture in Ethiopia, Book II. Publications and Foreign Languages Press Department, The Imperial Ethiopian Government, 1964, Addis Ababa, Ethiopia.

MoI, (1973), Ethiopia Today: Investment Opportunities, Ministry of Information, July 1973, Addis Ababa, Ethiopia.

MoLSA (Ministry of Labour and Social Affairs), (2012), National Social Protection Policy of Ethiopia, Final draft, Ministry of Labour and Social Affairs, 26 March 2012.

Proclamations

Declaration on Economic Policy of Socialist Ethiopia, (1975), Addis Ababa, Ethiopia, February 7, 1975.

Environmental Impact Assessment Proclamation No. 299/2002, Federal Negarit Gazette, 9th Year, No. 11, Addis Ababa, Ethiopia, 3rd December 2002.

Environmental Pollution Control Proclamation No. 300/2002, Federal Negarit Gazette, 9th Year, No. 12, Addis Ababa, Ethiopia, 3rd December 2002.

Expropriation of Landholdings for Public Purposes and Payment of Compensation Proclamation No. 455/2005, Federal NegaritGazeta, 11th Year No. 43, 15th July 2005.

Investment Proclamation No. 769/2012, Federal Negarit Gazette, 18th Year, No.63, Addis Ababa, Ethiopia, 17th September 2012.

Investment Proclamation No. 242/1966, Negarit Gazette, Addis Ababa, Ethiopia, 1966.

Labour Proclamation No. 377/2003, Federal Negarit Gazette, 10th Year, No. 12, Addis Ababa, Ethiopia, 26th February 2004.

Labour Proclamations No. 466/2005, Federal Negarit Gazette, 11th Year, No. 56, Addis Ababa, Ethiopia, 30th June 2005.

Labour Proclamation No. 494/2006, Federal Negarit Gazette, 12th Year, No. 30, Addis Ababa, Ethiopia, 29th June 2006.

Personal and Business Tax Proclamation No. 107/1949, Negarit Gazette, Addis Ababa, Ethiopia, 1949.

Proclamation No. 140/1954 to amend the personal and business tax proclamation no. 107/1949, Negarit Gazette, 14th Year No. 1, Addis Ababa, Ethiopia, 20th September 1954.

Proclamation No. 26/1975 for the ownership and control by the government of the means of production, Negarit Gazette, 34th year, No. 22, Addis Ababa, Ethiopia, 11th March 1975.

Proclamation No. 31/1975 for the public ownership of rural lands, Negarit Gazette, 9th April 1975, Addis Ababa, Ethiopia, The Provisional Military Administration Council.

Proclamation No. 47 of 1975 for government ownership of urban lands and extra urban houses, Negarit Gazette, 26th July 1975, Addis Ababa, The Provisional Military Administration Council.

Proclamation No. 269/2012 for the establishment of the Ethiopian Investment Agency, Federal Negarit Gazette, 19th Year, No. 2, Addis Ababa, 23rd November 2012.

Proclamation No. 803/2013 for the establishment of the Ministry of Environment and Forest, Federal Negarit Gazette, 19th Year, No. 61, Addis Ababa, 29 July 2013.

Proclamation No. 313/2014 for the establishment of the Ethiopian Investment Commission, Federal Negarit Gazette, 20th Year, No. 63, Addis Ababa, 14th August 2014.

Proclamation No. 283/2013 for the establishment of the Ethiopian Agricultural Investment Land Administration Agency, Federal Negarit Gazette, 19th Year, No. 32, Addis Ababa, Ethiopia, 4th March 2013.

Proclamation No.7/1992 for the establishment of National/Regional Self-government, NegaritGazeta, 51st Year, No.2,1992a, Transitional Government of Ethiopia, Addis Ababa, Ethiopia.

Proclamation of the Constitution of the Federal Democratic Republic of Ethiopia No.1/1995 – Federal Nagarit Gazette, 1st Year, No. 1, Addis Ababa, Ethiopia, 21st August 1995.

Regulations No. 10/1990 for the participation of foreign investors. Negarit Gazette, 49th year, No. 23, Council of Ministers, Addis Ababa, Ethiopia, 4th September 1990.

Regulations for the Establishment of Agricultural Development Corporations, Negarit Gazette, No. 21, Addis Ababa, Ethiopia, 20th February 1976; Negarit Gazette, No. 27, Addis Ababa, Ethiopia, 23rd March 1976.

Rural Land Administration and Use Proclamation No. 456/2005, Federal Negarit Gazette, 11th Year, No.44, Addis Ababa, Ethiopia, 15th July 2005.

Special Decree No. 17/1990 on Investment, Negarit Gazette, 49th year, No. 12, Council of State, Addis Ababa, Ethiopia, 19th May 1990.

Solid Waste Management Proclamation No. 513/2007, Federal Negarit Gazette, 13 Year No. 13, Addis Ababa, Ethiopia, 12th February 2007.

Index

For Product Safety Concerns and Information please contact our EU
representative GPSR@taylorandfrancis.com
Taylor & Francis Verlag GmbH, Kaufingerstraße 24, 80331 München, Germany

www.ingramcontent.com/pod-product-compliance
Ingram Content Group UK Ltd.
Pitfield, Milton Keynes, MK11 3LW, UK
UKHW020947180425
457613UK00019B/569

* 9 7 8 0 3 6 7 7 8 6 3 4 2 *